THE
JAPANESE
GARDEN

THE JAPANESE GARDEN

Photographs by Takeji Iwamiya

Text by Teiji Ito
Design by Yusaku Kamekura

Zokeisha Publications, Ltd., Tokyo

© 1972 by Takeji Iwamiya and Teiji Ito

Originally published in 1972 by
Yale University Press, New Haven and London;
and Zokeisha Publications, Ltd., Tokyo.

Second edition, 1978, Zokeisha Publications Ltd., Tokyo.

All rights reserved.
Library of Congress catalogue card number: 72-75196
International standard book number: 0-300-01601-8

The English text, written by Donald Richie,
is based on notes and manuscripts by Teiji Ito.

Printed in Japan by Zokeisha Publications, Ltd.
5-1-6 Roppongi, Minato-ku, Tokyo, 106

Contents

There are only two attitudes toward nature. One confronts it or one accepts it. The former finds in nature but the rawest of materials to do with as one will—a form is imposed upon chaos. The latter discovers in chaos a new kind of naturalness—and to naturalize nature is to accept it.

The histories of Western and Eastern gardens indicate these two attitudes, both supported by a philosophy and a metaphysics. In the Occidental garden, trees are ordered, paths are straightened, and a visible form is imposed. A person always knows where he is in such a place. He sees it from above, as it were. He will never become lost while taking a stroll because he, the lord of creation, has himself made his garden. Like his deity, he has crafted order from chaos and he feels himself somewhat god-like.

In the Oriental garden it is nature and not the gardener which does the creating. The line of a stone, the mass of a tree, the contour of a hillock—all of these things are observed and worked into a pattern which the garden architect has perceived, a pattern which, because it is natural, is unique. Since he is always inside his garden, the viewer is surprised by a new vista, an unexpected view—he arranges for it. His natural garden will change with the seasons, just as those who see the garden will change with the years.

Both kinds of gardens represent a kind of ideal. The Western garden represents ambition attained, nature subdued. It is an illustration of the humanist ideal: man is the measure of all things.

The Eastern garden and its assumptions are quite different. Man finally and firmly becomes a part of nature itself. There is no assumption that there is something better than nature. Nature is itself and that is enough. Though the Japanese have much to fear from nature— yearly typhoons, floods, earthquakes—they have also found much to respect. They have found, among other things, their own self-respect in recognizing that they are themselves a part of nature. The man who can accept nature can also accept himself.

This acceptance of self is something at which no Westerner can be said to have failed since so few attempt it. His way is different. He idealizes himself and, consequently, his natural surroundings. Hence his philosophical poise, his assurance, which, by its very grandeur, suggests aspirations inconsistent with acceptance.

To accept yourself completely you must also accept your own mortality, and this is what, somehow, and admittedly at an enormous expense, some Asians have been able to do. They can celebrate the changes of the seasons and still not feel that April is the cruelest month; they may contemplate the truly permanent with a dignity which does not allow easy if ironic thoughts of Ozymandias. Though sometimes sentimental and unusually given to the pathetic fallacy, the Japanese rarely allows the merely anthropomorphic to cloud his perhaps unique vision of the timeless.

This is because by sacrificing an urge to immortality, and through a knowing acceptance of himself and his world, he stops time. He has found a way to freeze it, to suspend it, to make it permanent. He does this, not through pyramids and ziggurats, but by letting it have its own way.

This is seen no better than in the Japanese garden where the seasons may change nature's skin, but the bones—rocks, water—are always visible, always unchanged. The Japanese garden is like a still picture—a frozen moment which is also all eternity. It remains the same no matter the season because the seasons are acknowledged, and this acknowledgment is spiritual, a combination of idea and emotion. As an old saying has it: ". . . gazing upon the mountain one's knowledge is widened; looking upon the water one's feelings are increased."

A mountain for intelligence, a lake for feelings; solid stone and fluid water. These are the antipodes of Asia. Its mountains and its seas are its only realities. Rocks to make mountains, waters to make oceans—the everyday stone and the commonplace pool allowed to express their natures, allowed to whisper their meaning. This is what the Japanese garden has been about from the beginning. It is a celebration of the elementals, a glimpse of nature bare, an analysis of the world in which we live.

One recognizes the feeling in Zen Buddhism, the influence of which upon the Japanese gardens, as we shall see, has been extreme. Just as Zen insists that one free oneself from this world of which one is a part by perceiving this oneness with the world, so the notion of nature seen in Japanese landscape gardening allows the forest to be seen despite the trees, the garden despite the rocks. Just as one, freed, may look upon and into oneself, so—in the garden—one sees an equally freed world, one which has been both physically reduced and spiritually enlarged to suggest the proportions of nature. With this nature, things as they truly are, as guide, one makes a garden which is not so much the ideal of a garden as the essence of a garden.

These gardens take many forms. In this way the history of Japanese gardens is at the same time the history of a metaphysic, of a philosophical concept. Some of these gardens have been far from the generalizations through which I have described the general landscape gardening concept in Japan. Just as there is many a Western garden—the 'romantic' garden of the nineteenth century, for example—which is distant from the formal European garden which I have used as antithetical to the Japanese, so there is many an early garden—the paradise garden, for example—which would seem to contain little of the salient Japanese attitude. Still, all of the gardens in this book indicate both a direction and an attitude.

And almost all of the various gardens still exist, and may be visited. One of the peculiarities of Japanese culture is that the new does not build directly upon the old but beside it, as it were. Just as one, in Kyoto, may travel from the tenth to the nineteenth and back to the fifteenth centuries simply by visiting temples, so one may observe in various gardens the history of gardening in Japan itself. The older and the newer continue to live, side by side.

In the same manner, the very different are reconciled in the Japanese mind. If gardens as different from each other as those in which the famous Golden Pavilion is situated, and the well-known Ryoanji rock garden, were found in the West, they might excite a categorization intended to account for styles so dissimilar. The Japanese aesthetic is somewhat different.

No comparative aesthetic is used. Instead, reconciliation is possible under an aesthetic rubric which finds all gardens—and many other objects of aesthetic consideration as well, for example, flower arrangement—subject to a single stylistic law.

The objects are either *shin* or *gyo* or *so*: that is, formal, ordinary, or informal. In practice, both gyo and so are created by using fewer elements of perhaps less excellent quality. These gardens turn out to be more symbolic than the shin garden. Akisato Ritoken, an eighteenth-century landscape architect, gives an example of this in his *Tsukiyama Teizōden Kohen*. If the 'complete' garden, filled with mountains, rocks, ponds, and so on, represents shin, then a garden with less actuality and some symbolism represents gyo, and the dry garden composed only of sand and rocks is so.

Or, the matter of stepping stones in the garden. Those with little space between them are deemed shin, and the stones themselves are artificially cut. The arrangement of either cut or natural stones with a bit more space between is gyo, and natural stones with a maximum of space is so.

This method of aesthetic codification and its terminology may seem far-fetched to the West—particularly in that its idea of formal would include the austere. It would be tempting to call the Ryoanji rock garden shin rather than so. However, this kind of categorization with its all-inclusive nature seems both natural and practical to the Japanese. Its assumptions are that the garden *is* nature and that these are three ways of viewing what already exists.

In the same way, another aesthetic concept, the *ten-chi-jin*, or 'heaven-earth-man' idea, which describes so much in Japanese art, implies that heaven is of this earth and that man is a part of the nature of this earth. Ikkyu, a fifteenth-century Zen priest, said that he loved the bamboo as his friend and that he respected water as his master. He belonged to this earth and accepted nature because, to his mind, there was no alternative to this acceptance. To this mind, the word 'beauty' means the beauties of nature. A 'beautiful flower' has always existed, but 'the beauty of a flower' cannot exist because the beauty cannot be abstracted from the flower.

Which is not to say that the beautiful flower or the beautiful tree is not to be improved upon. Ask a Japanese gardener the secret of gardening and he will hold up his pruning shears. But this pruning, called *sentei*, allows a more natural and, at the same time, more ideal beauty to emerge. The beauty is there from the first. It is not created, it is merely allowed to express itself in a louder voice and in plainer terms. The beautiful garden lives. The gardener merely makes this beautiful garden more visible.

In so doing he incorporates not only the visible lines, the rocks, the trees, he also makes visible the invisible, namely the effect that time will have upon the garden. He reckons the effects of the seasons on this garden he is releasing rather than creating; he calculates the life of the tree, the life of the stone. He does this not to evade these qualities but to incorporate them. He observes the laws of *mujo*, or mutability, and that of *seisei-ruten*, or the perpetual change of the universe. The garden lives. It grows, it changes. By incorporating into it the idea of change, the idea even of death, it triumphs over death itself—it is alive.

Such observance and acceptance of nature gave rise to an aesthetic theory of great importance. Just as everything is mutable, so everything is unique. There are no two things—trees, rocks—exactly alike. One does not strive for the perfect tree, for who is to say what perfection consists of in a world where each tree is different? Rather, then, one searches for the tree which clearly expresses its own unique individuality, for the rock which shows its difference.

In the same way, any composition which seems perfect, which shows a balance that could not be bettered, is of no use in a garden made up of objects the very identity of which must also suggest imperfection. To insist upon a harmony other than the underlying one naturally revealed in nature is, precisely, unnatural.

How the Japanese arrived at this concept is unknown. It has perhaps always been there. How it affects the kind of gardens they build, however, is the subject of this book. It is the history of an attitude, and through this becomes also a history of Japanese gardening itself.

The Japanese word for garden, *niwa*, suggests the origins of Japanese gardens. According to the *Daigenkai*, Japan's definitive etymological dictionary, the word was derived from *hanima*, literally a space of ground, but one set aside for special purposes.

In ancient literature—the *Kojiki* (712 A.D.), the *Wamei Ruijusho* (ca. 930)—niwa was the term used for the yard in front of the main halls of Shinto shrines or the Imperial Palace itself. In the *Nihon Shoki* (720) there is a record of a ceremonial procession around the year 470 which reads: ". . . a group of beautiful maidens walked elegantly in the *yuniwa* of the Asakura Palace in Hatsuse in Yamato."

This yuniwa, literally, a purified space of ground, may have been one of those broad yards covered with white gravel such as may still be seen in the Shishinden or the Seiryoden of the Imperial Palace in Kyoto. These empty yards, containing at the most a symbolic pair of trees, are like those completely empty gravelled courts in the confines of the Ise and other ancient shrines. Such gravelled courts, exorcised and hence sacred, were used to hold official and religious ceremonies and festivals. From the fourth to the sixth centuries—that is, through the Tumulus periods—the gravelled courtyard of the Imperial Palace was called yuniwa when used for Shinto rites, *oniwa* when used for state ceremonies.

The emperor was both temporal and spiritual leader of his country, and these first gardens reflect in their double uses his double role. Their progress into the form of garden which we know today might be explained, or at least illustrated, by the changing conception of the emperor system itself. Thus, as the emperor became more and more the temporal leader of his country from the end of the fifth century through the beginning of the sixth—during the period of the unification of the country and the establishment of a national government—the concepts of the yuniwa, that sacred and unadorned gravelled court, maintained only in shrines, and those of the imperial oniwa began to change.

Gradually, over the decades, trees, flowers, rocks, ponds made their appearance in this hitherto empty ground. Two of the reasons for this change in function in the oniwa were: first, the establishment of an aristocracy in this newly unified government, and second, the coming of Buddhism.

The new aristocrats had been provincial chieftains whose travels were confined to the mountains around Yamato, not too far from present-day Kyoto. As the government was formed, however, they travelled more and more widely, and saw much in nature which they had not known existed. These new aristocrats saw the further rivers, mountains—they saw the sea. Statesmen-poets writing poems later collected in the *Manyoshu* were particularly impressed with seascapes. Yamabe no Akahito (fl. 736) wrote with admiration of the view of Fuji from across Suruga Bay; Otomo no Yakamochi (fl. 785) praised Mount Tateyama in Etchu. Others travelled to remote Shikoku, or all the way to China, beginning and ending their voyages with a passage through the Inland Sea. Upon their return these early statesmen and warriors, poets all, wrote with nostalgia of the coasts and islands which they had seen.

It is supposed that it was in response to this nostalgia that the first gardens appeared. At any rate, these were simulated seascapes arranged in sections of the now completely secular oniwa. A portion of the traditionally white-gravelled courtyard was converted into a pond, representing the sea, with a pebbled shore about it. The pebbled variety was called *suhama*, literally 'gravelled seashore'; if stones were used, they were called *ariso*, or 'rocky beaches.'

Eventually, the garden itself became known as *shima*. Though this word meant and still means 'island,' from the mid-sixth to the eighth centuries (that is, from Asuka to Nara periods) it meant 'garden.' Around the middle of the seventh century one of the local ministers, Soga no Umako (d. 626), was nicknamed Shima no Otodo, or Garden-Island Minister, because in his Asuka villa he had a garden with a pond in which there was an islet.

The second major influence on Japanese gardens came through Buddhism, not so much from the creed itself as from the various aesthetic ideas which either came from Buddhist precepts or were introduced into Japan along with the religion itself.

One of the earliest of these records dates from 612 when a man named Roshi no Takumi —also known as Shikomaro—emigrated from Paekche in Korea. He was apparently well qualified as a gardener because he represented himself as being able to build miniature mountains. He actually did construct a model of the blessed Mount Shumisen (Sumeru) as well as a Chinese bridge, in the oniwa of the Imperial Palace.

This mountain, Shumisen in the Buddhist cosmology, was the center of the universe. It was the highest of all the mountains in the world. Roshi no Takumi's mountain was actually a large rock which he shaped, thus creating a garden vogue for artificial mountains. In 657 one was erected west of the Asuka Temple, in 660 another appeared at the end of the Isonokami Pond. In 1902 another was excavated in one of the Asuka villages of Nara. It was believed to have been the mountain erected on the river bank east of the Amakashi Hill, constructed for the garden of a local aristocrat. About ten feet tall, it consisted of three stones on the surface of which there was a design in relief indicating the folds of an ancient mountain.

As Buddhism brought into Japan many religious and aesthetic ideas, the garden grew and changed. When Prince Kusakabe (622–689) died, his courtiers eulogized their sorrow in over twenty poems of lamentation. In these they describe the garden of his palace, the Tachibana no Shimamiya in Asuka district. There was an artificial body of water known as 'the fragrant pond' about which water-fowl wandered; there was an auspicious red tortoise, given the prince by the Province of Suwa; around the sea-like pond there was a suhama and an ariso, and a Chinese-style bridge crossing to the island in the middle, while from the far end a footpath wound amid azalea bushes around the shore.

There were many other gardens as well during this early period. Tachibana no Moroe (684–757) made an elegant seascape garden around 752; Nakaomi no Kiyomaro made another around 758—both in the old capital, now Nara. What had happened in all of these early gardens, however, was that the original Japanese inspiration—simple nostalgic recreation of distant scenes, simple decoration for house and grounds—became more and more overlaid with the new and exotic ideas pouring in from China along with the new official religion, Buddhism.

From this early date, however, the Japanese genius for assimilation was well in evidence. The most incongruous elements, often coming from the most varied sources, are brought together and then gradually made to cohere in a manner which results in a style recognizably Japanese.

Those who complain that the Japanese do not originate miss the point. There are various ways of originating. The Japanese method is that of the oyster which collects its nacre, creating its pearl around the single grain of sand which it has appropriated. Just as the Japanese sees nature as a model and then simplifies it, forms it, allows it to reveal its intrinsic being, so foreign influences are mixed, metamorphosed. In later gardens we see this plainly: a harmonious mixing of things Japanese with things Chinese; with influences from native Shinto, influences from foreign Buddhism.

From the early island gardens of the Asuka and Nara periods came the later developments witnessed by the succeeding Heian era. These were, in large part, created by the architectural demands of the aristocrats who settled in the new capital of Heiankyo, a city founded in 797 and on the site of present-day Kyoto.

The type of architecture which evolved during this period is called *shinden zukuri*. It consisted of a complex of buildings, apparently originally arranged in a strictly symmetrical pattern. The center building was known as the shinden. Around it were three buildings: the *higashi-no-tai* (east hall), *nishi-no-tai* (west hall), and *kita-no-tai* (north hall). To the south were two more buildings, the *tsuridono* (pond pavilion) and *izumidono* (pavilion of the spring), both names of which suggest a more elaborate use of water than was theretofore common. All of these buildings were connected to one another with roofed bridges called *suiwa-taro*, and the *shinden* itself faced south, to the white gravelled courtyard and the pond beyond.

This earliest Japanese architectural style, so Chinese-influenced that it has been called 'T'ang with a difference,' is still to be seen: rebuilt, as in the Byodo-in at Uji near Kyōto, or copied, as in the Heian Shrine in Kyoto. Very beautiful and imposing hybrids they are, too, with sweeping T'ang roofs supported by graceful Japanese pillars. And just as this style incorporated Chinese lines above a Japanese foundation, so the original island garden was now overlaid by the very Chinese-influenced water garden.

The two went well together. From the gardener's point of view the combination was a natural one. Just as in Europe at a later date it was impossible to have a classical French or Italian garden without Greek architecture, so it was thought fitting that these seas and islands should exist within the kind of architecture that the Japanese thought the Chinese had.

These new houses and palaces were placed much nearer the lake than had been their presumed Chinese originals. Sometimes an entire structure (the tsuridono) was built directly over them, a style seen in such later edifices as the Gold Pavilion and the main shrine at Miyajima. One of the effects, or intentions, was to bring the building into the garden and the garden into the building, an idea which one might expect from the Japanese and their ideas on the intimate connections between man and nature.

The pond itself, which generally contained one or two islands, was fed by a stream which ran along the eastern side of the grounds. After feeding the pond, it emptied in a southwesterly direction. The effect was one of a profusion of water. The Chinese gardens, upon which these Japanese ones were presumably at least partially based, had lagoons and an occasional waterfall, but nothing like the streams and rivulets the Japanese insisted upon.

Aside from this, these new gardens might, at first glance, seem not too different from the original island gardens. There were, however, a few basic changes. In the island gardens each element within the garden was separate from every other, and the garden as a whole was organized so as to accentuate the contrast among heterogeneous elements. In these water gardens of the shinden-zukuri, however, each garden was in itself an entity, to be so observed, and the component elements were to be both consistent and harmonious.

This was fully accomplished when the influences from China ceased. The thirteenth envoy to the T'ang dynasty on the mainland was recalled in 838 and consequently less was heard from China. When something like this occurs, and it has at least several times in Japan's history, there is then a period of digestion, and eventually something in a style recognized as Japanese emerges.

This was visible in all the arts of the period. Painting, for example, was equally transformed. The Chinese style, known as Kara-e, became the Yamato-e, or Japanese style. Chinese influence was incorporated so thoroughly as to become invisible, and the result of this amalgam or series of amalgams became something uniquely Japanese. In gardens too —which, after all, represent a living approach to the same effects sought after in landscape painting—like changes occurred.

One of the ways in which they did so was, as always, through the Japanese appreciation of nature. A grand Chinese landscape was all very fine, but aristocrats enjoyed the landscapes in the suburbs of Heiankyo, as well as the more distant local sights. Just as the earlier Yamato aristocracy constructed seascapes remembered from the Inland Sea and further waters, so the titled and wealthy of the new capital began to make replicas of more domestic scenes in their gardens.

In one of them, the garden of the Kawara-in, constructed about 857 at the residence of one of the ministers, Minamoto no Toru, a scattering of islands suggested the famous beauty of Shiogama Bay in the province of Mutsu. In the garden of the Rokujo-in, at the residence of Ōnakaomi no Sukechika, there was a pond, and a long peninsula was constructed after the famous scenic spot of Amanohashidate in the province of Tango. In the garden of Taira no Shigechika, in the southern suburb of the city, there was a pebbled beach, or suhama, depicting the Sumiyoshi Beach in the province of Settsu.

Or, they constructed genre-gardens, ones in which no particular spot was recreated but rather, the air of the pastoral landscapes around the capital, those nearby spots to which the aristocrats repaired for parties and picnics. This style of garden was known as *nosuji*, literally suggesting 'a trail wandering in an elegant manner.' Along with the trail a stream usually wound its way through the garden, imitating a meandering countryside brook. Rocks were arranged along the stream in a manner which appeared natural, common wild flowers were planted, and local crickets were let loose in the bushes.

This view of nature touched up is one which the Japanese prefer above all others. Things are made, often most artfully, to look more real than real. An authentic landscape is much admired—and, even this early, Japan was already filled with celebrated scenic spots—but even more admired is the reproduction, the replica, nature contained. In this way, just as house and garden become interchangeable, yet one, so do man and nature.

Over and over one sees this approach to nature, not only in gardens but in literature, in painting, as well. The intended effect is pictorial and it is not surprising that many of the Yamato-e painters were also garden designers. Kose no Kanaoka, who lived at the end of the ninth century and is called the father of the Yamato-e, arranged the rocks for the Shisen-en, an imperial garden in the capital, as well as for other gardens in such places as the Kan-in and Daikakuji. His grandson, Kose no Hirotaka, a court painter, was also a garden designer. In the *Sakuteiki*, the early document on gardening published in the late eleventh century, he is cited as being particularly well up on garden taboos. Another painter of the period, Kudara no Kawanari (782–853) arranged the rocks of the *takidono* or 'waterfall house' at the Saga Residence. This relationship between landscape gardening and landscape painting was, indeed, so close that the same characters (山水, lit. 'mountain,' 'water') were used for both. Pronounced *senzui* it meant garden; *sansui*, landscape painting.

But there were other, and certainly equally important, influences assimilated during this period in the history of the Japanese garden. Among these were precepts, both Taoist and Buddhist, which had formed the context of Chinese ideas of landscape gardening and painting, and which the Japanese now modified. Two of the Taoist concepts were those of the *shijin-so* (four quarters) and the *furo-fushi* (immortal beings).

The 'four quarters' concept influenced the location of cities, villas, and cemeteries, as well as the character of gardens and their relation to architecture. The four sides of any area were assigned to four mythical creatures: east was given the Blue Dragon; south, the Red Phoenix; west, the White Tiger; and north, the Black Tortoise. Bearing these in mind, the architect of the well-located house made certain that there was a stream to the east, a pond to the south, a path to the west, and a hill to the north. This was the most auspicious of groupings, for then the four creatures could live happily together in environments congenial to them. This, in turn, meant that the residents would achieve power, wealth, and longevity. The Japanese, however, being innately practical, also had an alternate arrangement. If the stream and pond were impossible, the same effect could be obtained by planting nine willow trees in the east, nine Japanese Judas trees in the south, seven maple trees to the west, and three cypresses to the north.

Such concepts as these, torn from their Chinese contexts, and largely meaningless to the Heian nobility, were rigorously observed and later carefully codified. Tachibana no Toshitsuna, an eleventh-century landscape architect, wrote in the *Sakuteiki*: "The fortunate stream should flow from the east of the building along the south and then away to the west. By flowing in this direction, the stream will cleanse the evil air which exists in the ill-omened quarter (the northeast) and carry it away to the west. In this way, the household may enjoy a peaceful, long, and a healthy life, never suffering from disease or unhappiness."

One might note, however, that concurrent Buddhist thought insisted that the 'fortunate stream' flow in the opposite direction, from west to east, a concept supposedly derived from the historic eastward direction of Buddhist expansion. There are records of several such gardens including one made by a gardener named Matashiro, in which the eastward flowing 'fortunate stream' ended in a waterfall.

The other Taoist concept which helped shape Japanese gardens, that of 'immortal beings,' was introduced into Japan as early as the Nara period. These were spirits, entirely benevolent, who concerned themselves with such things as prosperity and, naturally, longevity. They were in the main social beings and looked after cities, families, and so on. During the middle of the Heian period, occasioned perhaps by the various upheavals which the country was beginning to experience, rumor went about that the immortals were leaving, and repairing to distant and blessed islands to enjoy an everlasting hermitage. This conceit, whether taken seriously or not, had a great effect on the gardens of the period, one which lasts also to this day. The nobles began to have artificial islands made in their gardens, giving them the names of the blessed isles, at least the three most important: Horai, Hojo, and Eishu. Believed or not, the idea was that finding such nice islands right here at home in the capital, the immortals would either refuse to leave or else could be persuaded to return.

At any rate, such representations began to be found in gardens. At the Toba Detached Palace, in the south of the capital, built for the retired Emperor Shirakawa (1053–1129), there

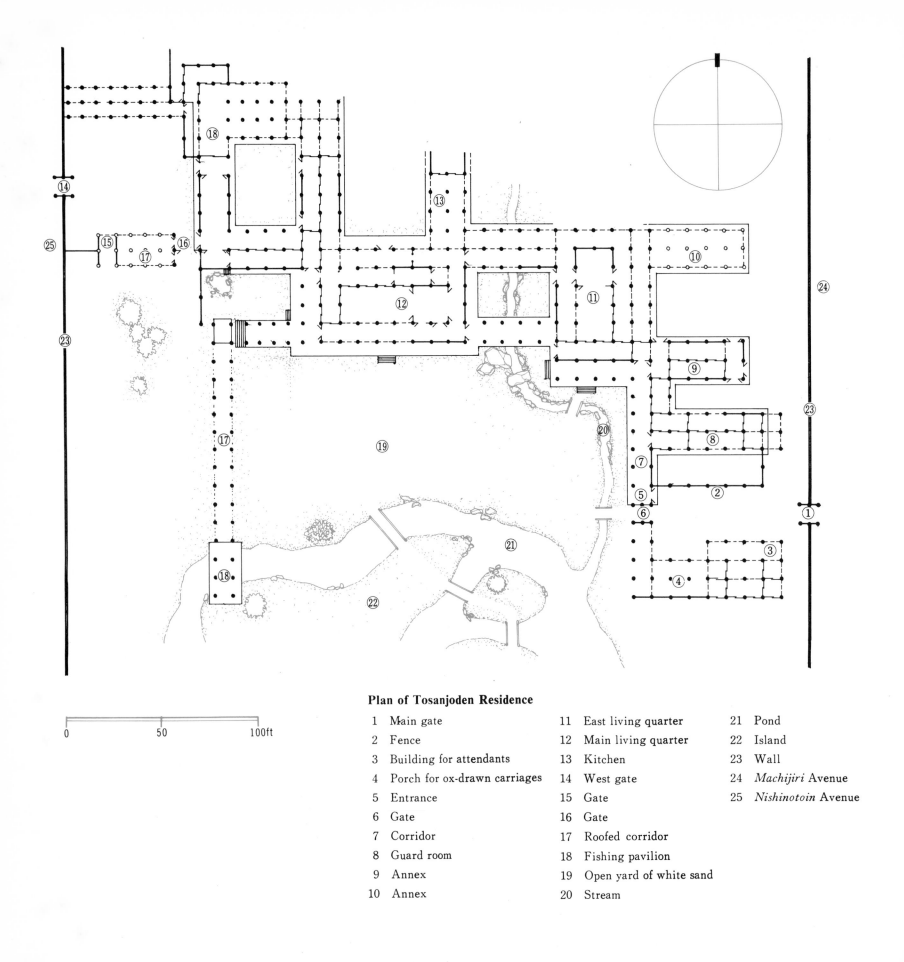

Plan of Tosanjoden Residence

1 Main gate
2 Fence
3 Building for attendants
4 Porch for ox-drawn carriages
5 Entrance
6 Gate
7 Corridor
8 Guard room
9 Annex
10 Annex

11 East living quarter
12 Main living quarter
13 Kitchen
14 West gate
15 Gate
16 Gate
17 Roofed corridor
18 Fishing pavilion
19 Open yard of white sand
20 Stream

21 Pond
22 Island
23 Wall
24 *Machijiri* Avenue
25 *Nishinotoin* Avenue

0   50   100ft

was an islet depicting one of the smaller immortal islands, Sokai, as well as a stone arrangement supposed to represent the mountain island of Horai itself. The famous warrior-statesman Taira no Kiyomori (1118–81) also had one of these mythical islands constructed in the garden of his official residence of Yomogitsubo in Kyoto.

The representation was not invariably that of an islet in a pond. At Tokai-an, in the monastery of Myoshinji, the priest Tomutsu simply dubbed a small hill in his garden an immortal island. Usually, however, the representation was fairly complete and a garden which had a complete set of all three isles was thought to be especially fortunate, because these three came to symbolize eternity itself. Several examples of gardens containing the set are those of the Nijo Castle in Kyoto, built by Kobori Enshu (1579–1647) in 1601, and the garden of the Sambō-in, a part of the temple complex of Daigoji built in the suburbs of Kyōto in 1598.

A further Japanese adaptation of the immortal isles resulted in the so-called crane-and-tortoise islands, both creatures reputed to enjoy a long life, and both certainly more familiar to the Japanese than blue dragons and white tigers. Just as the Japanese had perhaps originally found an excuse and an explanation for their fondness for watery island gardens in the legend of the immortals, so they now domesticated them by finding fancied resemblances to two of their native creatures. Not that the shape was important—the practice of putting out statues of real cranes and real tortoises is very recent. It was the designation which was important. Two extant examples may still be seen at the Rokuonji Temple, the old Kitayama Villa, much better known as the grounds of the Golden Pavilion, built in 1397 for the Shogun Ashikaga Yoshimitsu; and in the gardens of the Konchi-in monastery, built in 1632, in the Nanzenji compound in Kyoto.

Another example of Japanese adaptation was the use of pine. From the Nara period on in Japan (and in several other countries as well) the pine was a symbol of eternity—for obvious reasons: it never lost its green needles—and from the first was used on all the islands, immortal and crane-and-tortoise alike. It was also thought to go particularly well with that symbol for impermanence, for the transience of all earthly things—water itself.

Water was more important to the early Japanese than to other peoples. Certainly more was made of it. It was extensively used in early Shinto, and still is; it was referred to as 'purified' or 'holy'; it was used to keep evil spirits at bay. In the early capital there was also a plentitude of water. The Kyoto plain is a gentle slope comprised almost entirely of the ancient bed of the Kamo River, and studded with springs and natural fountains. In addition, the site of the capital is surrounded on three sides by mountains. In the summer there is little breeze and the hottest months are excessively muggy. Flowing water became important for another reason—as a means of controlling or at least lessening the temperature.

The importance of water to the Japanese may be judged by the number of words the language had for it—just as the importance of snow and camels may be judged by looking, respectively, into the Eskimo and Arab vocabularies. The *Sakuteiki* refers to ten different kinds of moving water. There was *mukaiochi* (from the sides toward the center); *hanare-ochi* (flowing among rocks); *tsutai-ochi* (flowing over rocks); *kata-ochi* (flowing to one side); *soba-ochi* (flowing at an angle); *nuno-ochi* (flat-flowing); *ito-ochi* (flowing in a thread-like pattern); *kasane-ochi* (flowing in a repeated pattern); *sayū-ochi* (divided by rocks into two streams); and *yoko-ochi* (flowing in cross currents).

Water was also used in various ways: the *izumi*, or spring; *yarimizu*, stream; *ike*, pond; *taki*, waterfall. In the shinden-zukuri architectural complex, the tsuridono is sometimes translated as 'fishing-hall,' and the izumidono was a building with, either actually or metaphorically, a spring. The three most famous of these 'spring halls,' alternately called *suikaku*, were: the Shirakawa Izumidono, built around 1100 as a part of the Toba Detached Palace; the Kuga Suikaku of Minister Minamoto no Norifusa, built around 1094; and the Hachijo Suikaku, built around 1097 for the governor of the Province of Bitchu.

The largest water garden, of which the pond still remains, was at the Shinsen-en, in the Imperial Garden of Kyoto, just south of the palace, and was constructed around the year 800. It is 720 by 1440 feet in size and contains in all 24 acres. The large pond has never gone dry, even during Kyoto's worst droughts. At the northeast corner was a spring from which the garden derived its name—the Sacred Spring Garden or, perhaps better, Garden of the Spring of the Gods. Originally the grounds were thickly wooded. Deer roamed freely and there were so many waterfowl that in one day's shooting in the year 836, as one journal reports, nearly 200 were bagged. There was a waterfall-hall or takidono near the mouth of the spring and, on the north side of the pond, the Kenrin Pavilion, one wing of which extended to form a fishing platform.

Another famous water garden was at the detached palace of the Emperor Saga (786–842), built around 814. Its pond alone was 5.6 acres in size, and was fed by a natural waterfall. Many of these water gardens, however, sooner or later went dry. The Jotomon-in fountain dried up in 1018, the Hachijo Suikaku fountain in 1097, and the fountain of the Higashi-sanjo in 1194. One of the reasons was that Kyoto was growing and available water was being used for the needs of the city. One of the consequences of this was that aristocratic Kyōto began to build in the south of the city where water was more plentiful.

Relatively little from the period exists. There are the ponds of the Shinsen-en in Kyoto, the pool of the Byodo-in at Uji, traces of the original gardens at Kinkakuji, the Temple of the Golden Pavilion, each one originally a self-conscious historical reconstruction. Perhaps the best idea of what they must have been is found in that excellent 1896 fantasy in the Heian manner, the Heian Shrine in Kyoto.

Another source, however, is the *Sakuteiki*, Japan's oldest book of gardening. Its author, Tachibana no Toshitsuna (d. 1094), was the illegitimate son of the Prime Minister Fujiwara no Yorimichi (992–1074) and could not, therefore, aspire to politics or government service. Perhaps consequently he became an artist and specialized in designing gardens. This book, the only one of his works to survive, is full of indications as to what these early gardens were, or should have been like.

The first chapter of the *Sakuteiki* is about shinden-zukuri gardens, and the author discusses at length the ponds, islands, streams, waterfalls, springs, bridges, and greenery necessary. He is extremely explicit on the various rules already formulated, rules so strong that should one break but one of them "the owner of the garden will sicken unto death; his residence shall also be laid waste, and shall become as the dwelling place of demons."

There were ten rules to be observed if this fate was to be avoided. Some had little to do with gardens or gardening. "It promises good fortune to irrigate the garden in the eastern quarter and to lead the water first to the south and then in a south-westerly direction. By so doing, all noxious airs will be washed away, and the master of the house will be cleansed of disease and malady and his life will be both long and full." Others had stronger aesthetic reasons behind them. Stones which had a grain or a shape which lent itself to standing erect should never be laid flat. Likewise, those stones which appeared more natural flat should never be stood up. "Else, these stones shall become ghost-stones and a curse will fall."

According to Toshitsuna, the three best contemporary water gardens were those at the Ishida Villa, and the Kaya Residence, and his own garden at the Fushimi Residence—all now gone. Citing these and other vanished gardens, Toshitsuna indicates not only the nature of these aristocratic pleasure-grounds, but also, as we have seen above, the philosophical and religious base upon which they rested and from which now other forms would grow.

Just as the evolution of the garden in the West expresses something of the post-Renaissance philosophy of Western man, so the Asian garden expresses the religions and philosophies of the East. Versailles, for example, is based upon the assumption that man is lord of the universe, that there is a place for everything, that everything is in its place, that earthly perfection may be expressed in terms of geometry. Loss of this assurance, and a consequent gain in understanding, is reflected in the more natural looking gardens of the late eighteenth and early nineteenth centuries in France and England.

In the same way, assumptions and beliefs are reflected in Japanese gardens of earlier periods. It was the Esoteric Buddhism of the Heian period which gave the garden its philosophical model. Though this influence began late, some four hundred years after Buddhism had been introduced into the country, it provided a basis strong enough to be glimpsed even now.

In Esoteric Buddhist theory, all things in nature are considered as *mandala*, literally 'pictures of the Buddhas,' that is, embodiments in reality of the spiritual world. The codification is extreme. The arrangement of buildings within the precincts of a temple, the order of statues in a temple hall, all express a mandalistic cosmos. The arrangement of all elements in space symbolizes the structure of an esoteric and otherwise *invisible* spiritual world. This is not one of the ways of seeing, it is *the* way of seeing *the* world.

Conventionally, the mandala takes the form of a painting, a hanging, containing a large number of illustrations in which the many Buddhas are arranged. This includes, almost invariably, the *dainichi-nyorai* (maha-vairocana), the principle of Esoteric Buddhism itself, but there are differences in the patterns. The *kongo-kai* (vajradhatu) is different from the *taizo-kai* (garbhadhatu) since these are, in themselves, two worlds which, in the words of Papinot, are "destined to help man find the origins of soul and body, in order to purify all his actions and thus, without limit in the illumination of the Buddha, arrive at virtue and happiness."

These two worlds insist upon a geometric regularity of pattern, but what is important is not this regularity but, rather, the way in which the elements of the various mandala interrelate. Thus, when the gardens of temples or residences were made according to mandalistic concepts, geometric regularity was not reflected or considered in any way necessary. Paintings and hangings might arrange themselves in circles or squares because their surfaces were two-dimensional. Gardens, like sculpture, could disregard surface pattern, approaching a freedom of form which would better conceptually illustrate a religion which was attempting to make believers aware of an inner existence through spatial composition.

Another, and much more popular, reading of the Buddhist mandala was that it simply represented paradise or, at least, a world better than this one. As in early Chinese gardens, as in European gardens and those of the Near East, the idea of a garden as somehow the reflection of a better world is a strong one—one, also, which is usually resisted by the Japanese, convinced as they often are that no better world exists, that, at least, nature is in itself a kind of ideal.

Occasionally, however, Japan too feels the need for a better world than this. This attitude was particularly strong during the closing years of the Heian era. It was a period of bitter civil war, of disillusion and destruction. Social order, even life itself, became less and less secure. Human life was like a snowflake which 'melted, thawed, resolved itself into a drop of dew'; life was as short, as fleeting as a floating bubble—an image used by a man of that period, Kamo no Chomei (1153–1216), in his essay, *Hojoki*. Mutability, constant change—this was native feeling acknowledged as the very essence of our life in this world, and a view which the times forced and which Buddhism upheld.

To the Japanese, eternity was, and remains, a pattern of change, and to the Japanese artist, the garden with its variously changing aspects was a symbol of this eternity. The garden, like life, was mutable. A geometric garden, or one which disregarded nature's quality of change —this concept did not occur to the Japanese. Immutability was death itself; only the changing was alive.

At the same time, however, the appeal of an earthly paradise was very strong. Mutability is the way things are, but how nice if there were also a paradise. This was a feeling experienced by these early Japanese, one encouraged by Esoteric Buddhism which was full of such concepts of *enri odo* ('to leave this detestable world') and *gongu jodo* ('to seek for paradise'). After death all desired to live in this better world, to be saved by Amitabha, the lord of paradise himself. Which, of course, is one of the reasons for the growth of the paradise garden itself during this period. If one owned a replica of paradise in one's backyard, as it were, the real one was that much closer.

The mandalistic paradise consisted of seven parts: a *bugaku-e* or place for music and dance; a *raibutsu-e* or place for the saints; a *hochi-e* or treasure pond; a *juge-e* or holy place under the trees; a *sanzon-e* or place for the Amitabha in triple-form; the *horo-kyuden-e* or treasure hall, and the *koku-e*, a gathering place for the angels, holy animals, and so on. These parts, though often arranged in a circle or other geometrical form, were meant to be seen as a complex whole without beginning or end, with no chronology, an entity which, given the conventions of painting, was meant to be viewed from above—a bird's-eye view of the spiritual world. The eye was to embrace at one instant all of the felicities of this paradise—from the place for music and dancing where the blessed naked children joined the dancing Buddhist saints to the kokū-e, where saints and angels play endlessly on musical instruments, where horses fly through the air, and where the sky is filled with falling flower petals.

Since the ideal view was from above, these temple complexes and gardens were also designed as though to be viewed from the air. The paradise garden in the Byodoin (ca. 1053), the Joruriji (ca. 1170), the Enjoji (ca. 1153), Motsuji (twelfth century), and Shomyoji (ca. 1256) all show the same pattern, though there are minor compositional differences. The main hall is the treasure hall, the lotus pool in front is the hochi-e, the bridge over it symbolizes the *guzei*, that bridge over which the blessed are led into salvation. The island in the pond is the place for the Amitabha in triple form, and so on. The compositions from eye-level are accidental; those from a hypothetical and unrealizable view from above are planned.

The same is, to be sure, true of classical European gardens. Laid out in squares, rectangles, triangles, they demand a bird's eye for fullest contemplation of the pattern. The assumptions of European and Asian gardens, however, are quite different. The former is made of straight lines and geometric shapes because this seems logical to the logical mind, and the ideal is a mathematical ideal. The ideal of the Japanese mind is metaphysical. Just as one perceived the structure of the garden through an interpretation of its mandalistic intention, so one perceived with the inner eye of understanding its ideal view from above.

To merely look at the paradise garden would make its difference from earlier gardens seem small. Actually, however, there are a number of differences. One of the more important is that though the pond looks somewhat the same in both, the representation is different. In the water garden it is the sea; in the paradise garden it is an aspect of the Buddhist paradise. Around this paradisical pool grew iris, willow, lotus, and other plants not to be found on any seacoasts, real or imagined. There are technical differences as well. There is no meandering stream or wandering path. One does not approach the pool from the east or the west, only from the south.

Another and more important difference is aesthetic. The early water garden is a whole, a pastoral scene. The later paradise garden is in itself a complex of parts. Though, ideally, the mandala when painted and hung was to be viewed in an instant, the garden, by its nature, had to be experienced in sections. Though the garden was to have been seen from a fixed point—directly overhead—it was in actuality experienced as a series of events. In the Catholic church there are the stations of the cross; in mandalistic Buddhist construction, architecture as well as garden, there are the various parts of an imagined paradise.

This difference in aesthetic outlook was to be of primary importance in later developments of the Japanese garden since it was this new way of looking at the garden which eventually resulted in the intention that the garden be viewed while strolling through it.

Yet another difference was the growing confusion between temple and residential architecture and landscape gardening. Sometimes villas were converted into temples. Sometimes privately owned temples became residences. The Fukushoin (1151) had its sacred hall directly connected to the residential buildings. The Sanjo-Shirakawa-bo (1235) had buildings for the liturgy connected with laymen's residences. Conversely, the Hojoji (1019) was originally the town house of the chief advisor to the emperor, Fujiwara no Michinaga; the Byodo-in at Uji was the villa of another advisor, Fujiwara no Yorimichi; the Shomyoji (1332), near Yokohama, had been the villa of Hojo Sanetoki, a regent in the Kamakura government.

One of the results of this integration of temple and residential architecture was that the paradise garden, originally a religious garden or, at least, one with religious connotations, became gradually more and more secular. It combined itself once more with the water garden, but a further metamorphosis created during the Kamakura (1185–1392) and Muromachi (1392–1572) periods another form of garden, a later form of the paradise garden. The differences of the paradise gardens of the Heian era as compared to those of the Muromachi are to be observed in the garden of Saihoji.

This temple is today also known as the Kokedera, because of the moss which so luxuriantly covers the lower garden. Actually, the moss is recent, the result of the neglect of the garden during the Meiji era (1868–1911), when the temple was too poor to keep the garden up. It was originally one of the more splendid of the paradise gardens and one can still trace and reconstruct the original fourteenth-century form.

The garden was built in 1339, paid for by Fujiwara no Chikahide, a powerful member of the Ashikaga government, and designed by a Zen priest, Muso Soseki (see below). The garden was much larger then; it extended all the way from the bottom of the mountain to the top. At the bottom was the *ogonchi*, or golden pond, which still exists, and at the top were a number of pavilions. The central hall, the *shariden*, was on the west side of the pond, an elegant building which was to become the model for both the Golden Pavilion at the Kitayama residence and the Silver Pavilion at the Higashiyama villa.

The differences from the Heian paradise gardens are many. They were arranged with component buildings in a determined course, usually east to west. In the Muromachi gardens the buildings were distributed much more freely and were more separate from each other. One of the results was that mandalic Buddhist assumptions were weakened. Rather than seeing the garden as a visible delineation of an ideal and interior Buddhist paradise, one saw nature itself. This was not so much a reversion to the native animistic beliefs of Shinto as it was an advance toward aesthetic enjoyment for its own sake.

Present Plan of Saihoji Temple

1 *Saihoji* river
2 Bridge
3 Main approach
4 Priests' living quarter
5 Buddhist hall
6 *Shonantei*
7 Footpath
8 Pond
9 Site of former *Ruriden*
10 Site of former *Tanhokutei*
11 *Kojokan* gate
12 Stone arrangement
13 *Shitoan*
14 *Ryuensui* Spring

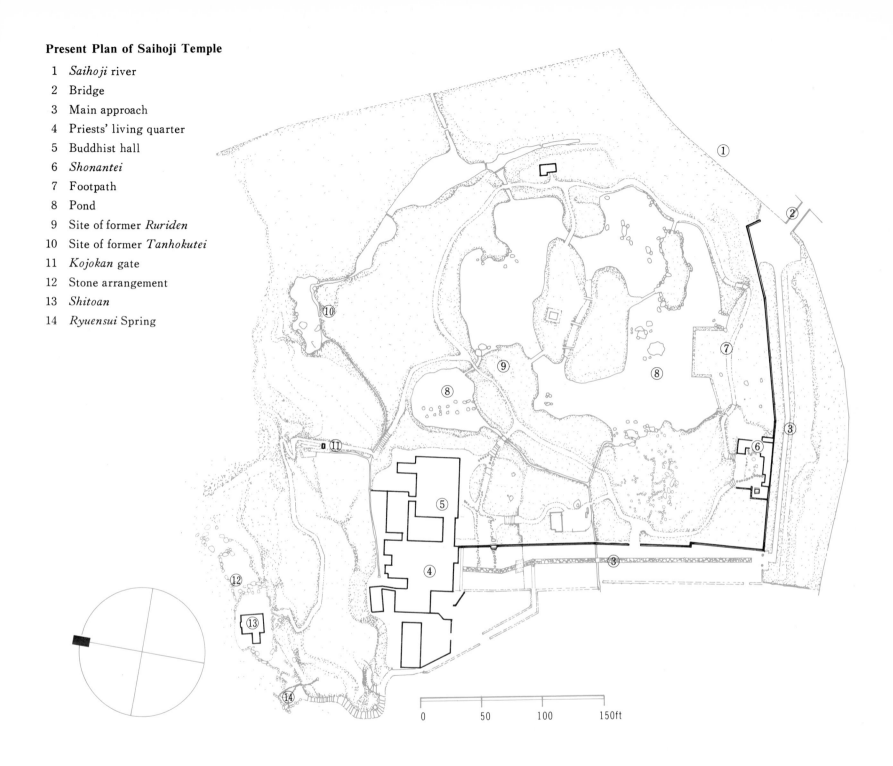

Another paradise garden was that of the Kitayama residence, the garden of the Golden Pavilion. It was built in 1397 for the Shogun Yoshimitsu (1358–1408) on the grounds of the mountain villa of the Saionji family, upon the site of an early paradise garden originally built by Saionji Kimitsune, a court noble of the earlier period.

Yoshimitsu, an aesthete who was steeped in the older Heian culture, rebuilt the garden using as a model the garden at Saihoji. There were a number of scattered buildings, both sacred and secular. There was a *gomado*, a hall where the sacred fire was lighted, but there was also the Kansetsu-tei, a small pavilion where one sat to admire the snow. The most important of the buildings—a replica is still standing, the original having been destroyed by fire in 1954—is the shariden, the famous Golden Pavilion.

Though this building has sometimes been compared to the Phoenix Hall of the Byodoin, built in the Heian period, there is little resemblance. The Golden Pavilion is not integrated into the landscape. It has little mandalistic intent. It is simply an informal and beautiful structure by the edge of the water. The first floor is a conscious reconstruction of a Heian residence and was used for recreations such as parties, poetry gatherings, theatrical performances, and so on. Called a Buddhist hall, it was rarely used as such—indicating the great differences between the Heian and Muromachi periods.

Another example is the garden at the Higashiyama villa, the Jishoji, the principal attraction of which is now the famous Silver Pavilion. It was built by the Shogun Yoshimasa (1435–90) around 1482. It is now difficult to recognize the components of the paradise garden, due to seventeenth century reconstructions, but the treasure pond is easy enough to identify, and, since this was a climbing garden, one may imagine various buildings scattered here and there, creating an earthly rather than heavenly paradise.

One of the results of a religious concept's becoming secular is that aestheticism takes the place of the original faith. Though the Muromachi gardens retained their concern with Buddhist traditions, and though the mandala pattern remained occasionally visible, the interpretations were, as we have seen, far different. Aesthetic enjoyment became more and more the function of the garden. One may then see these Muromachi-period gardens as the midway point between the early religious Heian gardens and the later gardens of the Edo period, meant to be walked in, meant to be enjoyed, in which religious inspiration played no part, and where aesthetic enjoyment was the complete aim.

The men partially responsible for these changes were themselves priests since it was they who were the first garden designers. From the later Heian period through the beginnings of the Kamakura era, both temple and residential gardens required designers with a knowledge of Esoteric Buddhism. Such priests were called *ishitate-so*, literally, priests who arrange stones.

History has retained many of their names. At the Ninnaji, where a number of such gardener-priests resided, several of their number compiled or wrote the second of the great Japanese garden treatises, the *Senzui narabini Yagyo no Zu*, or "Pictorials of Mountains, Water, and Landscape," the single extant copy of which dates from 1448. They also arranged the stones and designed the water course for the garden of the Hirano Shrine in 1204. One of their group—judging from his name, Seigen—designed the garden at Yofukuji, built in 1189 for Minamoto no Yoritomo (1147–99). Hogen Seii, an official court priest, together with another priest named Rinken built the garden at the Hokongo-in in 1130. In 1230 Fujiwara no Teika (1162–1241) appointed one Shinjakubo, a gardener-priest from Saga, to plan the garden of his Kyogoku residence. He noted in his diary that "the arrangement of

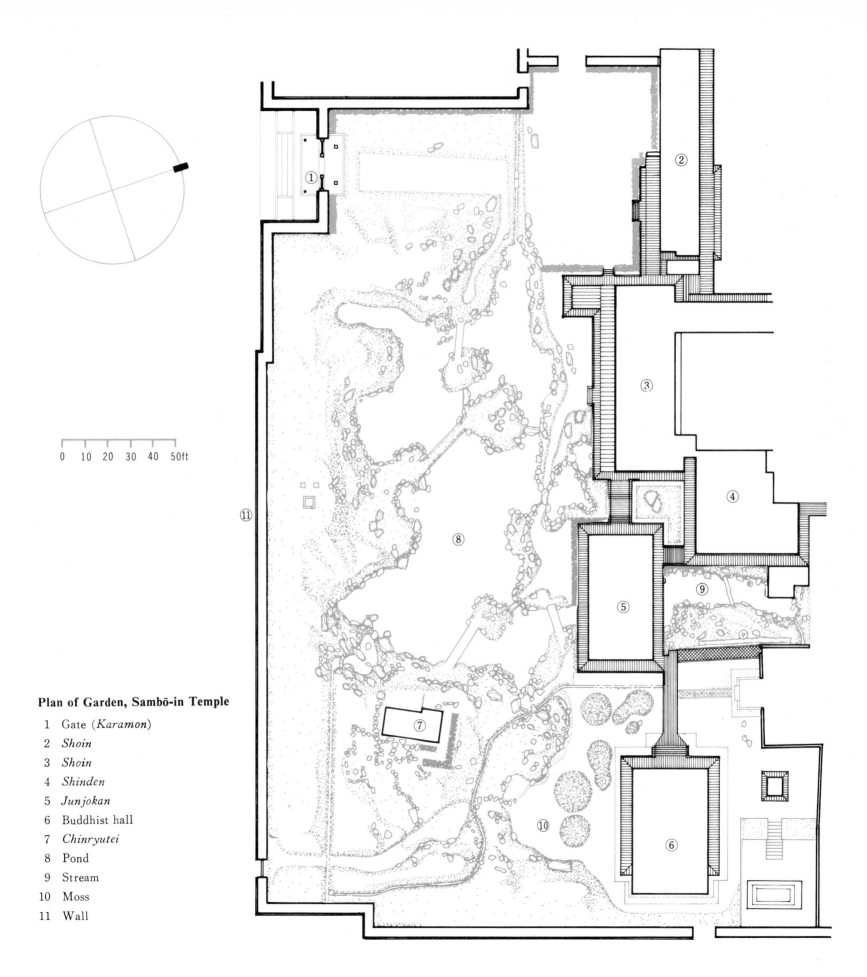

Plan of Garden, Sambō-in Temple

1 Gate (*Karamon*)
2 *Shoin*
3 *Shoin*
4 *Shinden*
5 *Junjokan*
6 Buddhist hall
7 *Chinryutei*
8 Pond
9 Stream
10 Moss
11 Wall

0 10 20 30 40 50ft

25

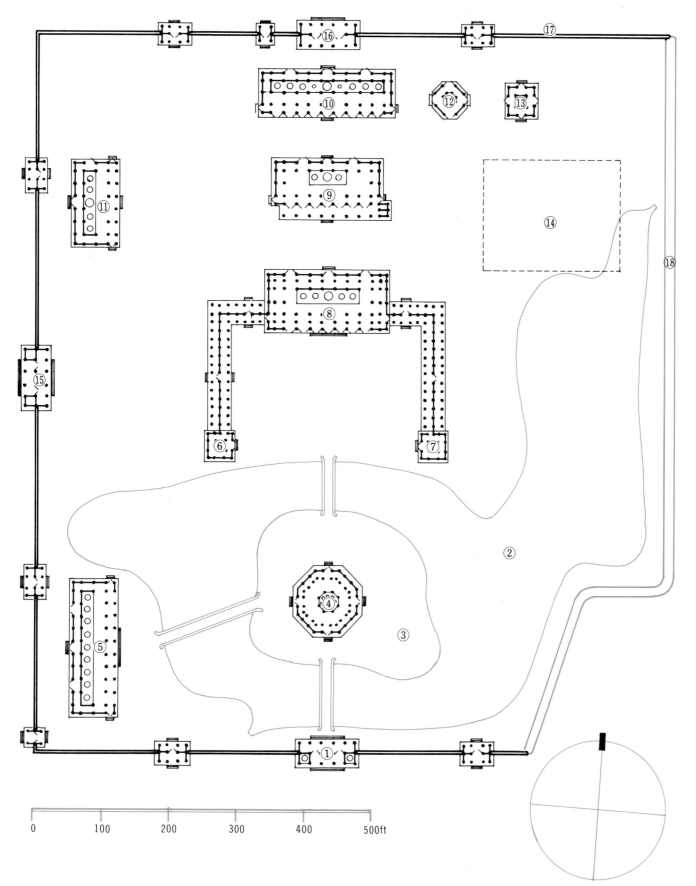

Plan of Hoshoji Temple

1 Main gate
2 Pond
3 Island
4 Nine-storied pagoda
5 Amitâbha hall
6 Bell tower
7 Sutra library
8 Main hall
9 Lecture hall
10 Bhêchadjaguru hall
11 Five Great Raja hall
12 Octagonal hall
13 Lotus hall
14 Residence
15 West gate
16 North gate
17 Wall
18 Mound

plants and trees was left entirely to the discretion of the priest." Another priest, Shingyobo, worked from 1255 to 1267 constructing the garden of Eikyuji. One Shoichi made the paradise garden of the Jomyoji in the early fourteenth century; one Jishin did the garden at Daijiji.

The greatest as well as one of the last of these gardener-priests was Muso Soseki (1276–1351), who designed many gardens, among them those of Saihoji, Nanzenji, and Tenryuji, all in Kyoto, that of Gyukoji in Tosa, and Yorinji in the province of Kai. He further played an important part in the transition which occurred in garden architecture.

He was a Zen priest and one of the canons of Zen was a gradual denial of Buddhist art, particularly the simplicities implicit in the mandalic religious philosophy. Just as Zen teaches one to be in harmony with one's own nature, so its creations—ink paintings, gardens—presume a oneness with nature which is much more sympathetic to the Japanese character than were Chinese-influenced precepts of Esoteric Buddhism as popularized by the mandala concept. Though of extremely high rank—his priestly title, *kokushi*, was granted him by the emperor himself—he was bitterly criticized for his increasing secularism. Goho, a priest of the Esoteric sect, was particularly forceful. "It is degenerate," he said, "for a leading priest to construct gardens under a pretense that they are based upon the precepts of Zen Buddhism." One of his reasons may have been the feeling that only lower-rank priests should bother themselves with garden construction; another may have been the natural rivalry between the Zen and Esoteric sections; yet another—and one, certainly, important to the history of Japanese gardens—may have been the feeling that under the influence of Zen, the garden was departing further and further from orthodox Buddhist precepts and turning—as, indeed, it was—into a place of pure aesthetic enjoyment.

Called *kara-senzui* (literally, 'dry garden'), this form of landscape architecture, which Zen Buddhism was to elevate to the highest importance, appears to have been in existence even during the Heian period, where it existed side by side with the water gardens of the time. According to the eleventh-century *Sakuteiki* manual, the kara-senzui was already a general term meaning a garden without water, one consisting entirely of stones.

There were apparently a number of types. One represented a pastoral scene, another a rustic town in the mountains, another the mountains themselves, and so on. The Muromachi dry gardens departed from this Heian concern with simple scenes. They grew symbolic. This metamorphosis, an interesting reversal of the direction we have seen between the water garden and the paradise garden of these same two periods, was due almost entirely to the influence of the Zen philosophy.

According to Zen, all of the phenomena of the universe are embodiments of the reality in Buddhism: all things in nature are also figures of the Buddha. To the Zen priest, the sound of the river, the waterfall, the wind in the pines—all are compared to a continuous and everlasting reading of the sutras. In the same way, mountains, stones, trees, grasses show in their shapes the true appearance of the Buddha. For this reason even the earliest Zen had no use for mandalistic thought, just as it had no use for the carved statues of the Buddha which other sects found necessary. Originally, Zen denied all religious art. According to the Esoteric doctrine, the garden must be a mandalistic paradise to be a religious garden; according to Zen precepts a garden might dispense entirely with the mandalistic pattern and be no less truly Buddha's.

Consequently, Zen architecture and Zen gardens lost—to the conservative eye of Esoteric Buddhism—the very spirit of the Buddha. During the Muromachi period, for example, the orthodox way of hanging the necessary three scrolls, the *sanzon-bosatsu*, or three holy Buddhas, was to show the main personification of the Buddha flanked on one side by Monju, a Buddhist saint of wisdom and intellect, and, on the other, by Fuken, another Buddhist saint. In the thirteenth century, however, there is the record of a triad of scrolls hung by a Zen priest named Mokkei at Daitokuji. In the center was Kannon, the so-called Goddess of Mercy. This deity was flanked on one side by monkeys and on the other by cranes. To these charming creatures was entrusted the role of interpreter of the universe. Monju (monjuri) and Fuken (samantabhadra) were deposed; nature in the form of its birds and animals might speak directly.

Or, deity might be revealed as nature itself. In Zen stone arrangements the stone became the deity, not to be worshipped as such, of course, but to be, as it were, symbolic of the deity always present in nature. The sanzon-bosatsu in Zen gardens took the form of three stones. The tallest middle rock was Shakyamuni, or the Buddha, and the other two were Monju and Fuken. No longer was any pictorial delineation necessary. The religious personages revealed themselves as already a part of nature. They became symbolic not in the Western sense of taking the place of, but in the sense of 'standing for' or indicating.

Around the three sanzan-bosatsu stones at both Rokuonji and Daitokuji are a number of other stones which 'stand for' the sixteen *rakan* or disciples. There are many stones called (rather than named) Kannon (Avalokitesvara) or Fudo (Acalanatha), the stone itself becoming a symbolic representation.

One of the reasons for the transformation of the paradise garden at Saihoji was that Muso Soseki was a Zen priest who denied religious art, who insisted that the same spirit was better seen in nature itself. Thus all of these now anonymous rocks originally had names. His garden was, nominally, as it were, Buddhist. It was, however, primarily, also a place where nature was both preserved and apprehended. The garden itself, rather than the names given the rocks, was an illustration of the Zen doctrine of the universality of the Buddha. The reason for the adoption of stones, sand, and little trimmed shrubs as architectural elements in dry gardens is that in Zen philosophy one is led to spiritual awakening by intuition through looking at the most primitive or simplest elements composing nature—the simpler in expression, the deeper in content.

After the middle of the fifteenth century, Zen—itself passing from the conservative Sorin school to the progressive Ringe school—became the aesthetically controlling influence. It was a period of great social unrest, of wars and revolutions, and it continued for more than a century. The capital was destroyed and the very foundations of life seemed in danger. With the visible destruction of social order came a necessary loss of belief in the measured philosophical order implied in Esoteric Buddhism. Only Zen, itself attuned to the natural both in man and nature, seemed to have any religious or philosophical meaning. A religion which aspires toward a spiritual peace becomes more and more important in an era from which peace, social or personal, is missing.

Thus, under the influence of Zen, the spiritual life of Japan advanced in the very midst of increasingly severe wars and revolutions. It was during this period that the arts of contemplation, that of the tea ceremony, the flower arrangement, the Nō drama, attained their most perfect form. Akin in spirit to these contemplative arts was the dry garden.

Just as the tea ceremony and flower arrangement make frugality a virtue, creating with the simplest of means a world of stillness and beauty, so the dry rock garden, in the smallest of areas, created an ideal landscape, a garden for the mind.

In 1466, when a Zen priest named Shinzui saw a small rock garden which Zenami had created at the Suiin-ken residence, he said that he became lost in reverie and completely forgot to go home, that "one can never tire of looking at such a garden." There was no need for nearly nine acres, no need for the intricacies of the gardens at Saihoji or the Kitayama residence. A Zen priest named Tessen Soki, the man who designed the garden at Unuma in the prefecture of Mino, and who may have built the famous stone garden at Ryoanji, spoke in his garden book, the *Ka Senzui no Fu*, of the art of "reducing thirty thousand miles to the distance of a single foot."

An entire world was created in a tiny plot of ground. In the garden to the east of the main hall at the Daisen-in temple, built by the priest Kogaku Sokokan in 1513, the total area is one hundred and thirty square yards, yet it contains more than one hundred stones set against white sand. It begins with a suggested waterfall and ends with an assumed ocean. There are bridges and boats for the imagination. At the same time, such symbolism is not insisted upon. It is, equally, an object for purely aesthetic contemplation.

In Zen Buddhism one does not seek to analyze the truth. Rather, one grasps the truth as a whole. "Not logically, but intuitively," goes the phrase, "does one seek the truth." This spiritual ideal presumes an awareness and acceptance of the entire universe. The dry garden with its sand and stones is a kind of Zen lesson. It is a garden abstracted, a world created in all of its diversity, yet unified. It is not realistic because it is real. It goes one step beyond the expected and moves toward the ideal. Each element in it is natural, yet this combination of elements is an embodiment of Zen philosophy, a model of Zen thought.

The most famous example is the stone garden at the Ryoanji. It is less than four hundred square yards in size, and within its rectangle of sand fifteen stones are distributed. On two sides, the west and the south, are low walls; on the north and east sides are parts of the temple. It is austere, unchanging, endlessly fascinating.

Though the stones may be explained, as they have been, as a mother tiger and her cubs crossing the sea, or as a seascape, the sand being the shallow ocean, the rocks, the island, or as a mystical embodiment of the idea of the trinity at the heart of all Buddhism—the fact remains that these rocks are also what they are, neither more nor less.

The Japanese garden is here far from the naturalism of the Heian seashore garden. It is equally far from the sometimes facile symbolism of the paradise garden. Ryoanji's garden is the ideal of a garden, it is the living blueprint of the perfect garden.

Though many dry gardens used moss, grass, even trees, as well as sand and stone, it was the stones themselves which were considered important. The Taizo-in abbot's residence at the Myoshinji has a dry garden which faces trees and shrubs; the south garden of the abbot's residence at the main hall of Daitokuji (ca. 1636) has an island of moss and stones seen against a background of trees; in the east garden of the abbot's residence at the Shinju-an (ca. 1638),

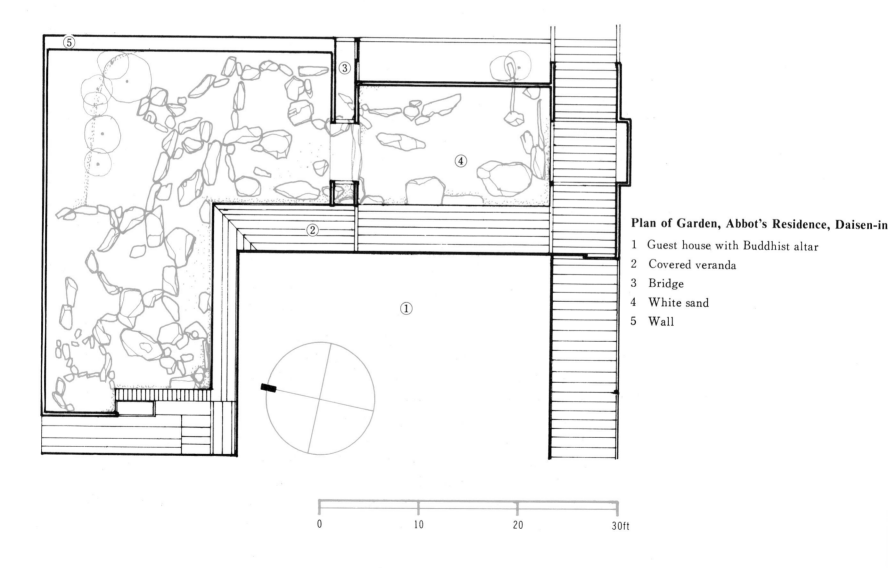

Plan of Garden, Abbot's Residence, Daisen-in

1 Guest house with Buddhist altar
2 Covered veranda
3 Bridge
4 White sand
5 Wall

0   10   20   30ft

and at the garden of Entsuji (ca. 1650), stones are scattered over moss and amid trimmed bushes. In all of these gardens it is acknowledged that the stones and not the greenery make the garden what it is.

The art of stones, which reached its height during the Muromachi period, came naturally to the Japanese. With their intuitive feeling for nature, with the original Shinto religion—animism itself, spirits inhabiting waterfalls, trees, rocks—with their love of natural patterns, natural textures, it would have been surprising if this feeling for rocks had not developed into an art.

Usually granite and andesite were most admired. Since the art does not consist of piling up stones one on another, however, absolute hardness was not a requisite. Much more important was the shape and texture. A whole aesthetic was built upon these. The weathered texture of certain stones was much admired, and was referred to by the aesthetic term *sabi*, which might be translated as 'patina.' Stones from the mountains had *yama-sabi*, those

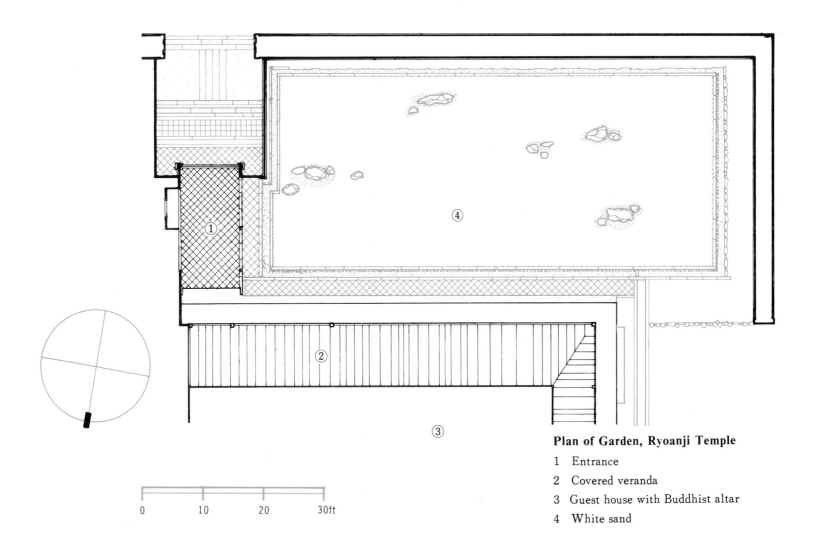

Plan of Garden, Ryoanji Temple

1 Entrance
2 Covered veranda
3 Guest house with Buddhist altar
4 White sand

0   10   20   30ft

Plan of Abbot's Residence, Taizo-in

1 Entrance
2 Covered veranda
3 Guest house with Buddhist altar
4 White sand
5 Moss
6 Low hedge
7 Island
8 Dry pond (white sand)
9 Dry stream (white sand)

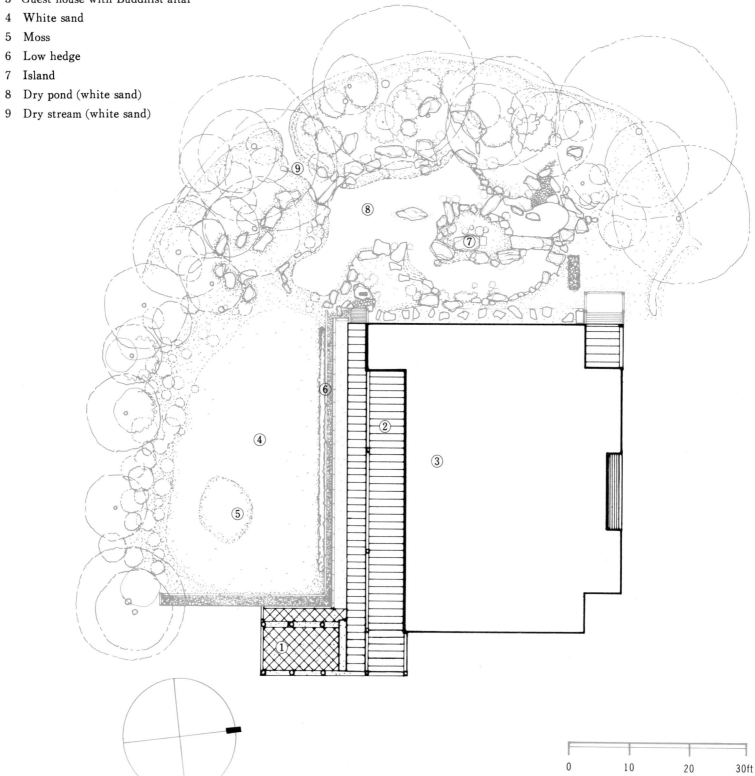

0   10   20   30ft

from the shore had *hama-sabi*, and so on. The shape preferred was that in which nature had created them.

Overlaid upon this native aesthetic was another drawn from classical painting. Just as earlier landscaping had much in common and owed much to landscape painting, so stones such as those appearing in earlier Chinese and Japanese paintings were preferred—a fact clearly indicated in the seventeenth-century book of garden and stone drawings, the *Kaishien Gaden*.

Such stones were not to be highly colored, though the occasional deep color found in water-stones was thought well of. At the same time, not all of a stone was to be admired. The bulk was often buried, leaving only the desired portions above ground. This was thought to give the feeling of stability—the greater the invisible portion of the stone, the more the feeling.

There was, in addition, an entire aesthetic of stone grouping. The assumption was that a desired harmony was almost impossible if even and balanced groupings were insisted upon. In a manner directly the opposite of Western garden aesthetics, the Japanese insisted upon asymmetrical or odd-number groupings. Six stones, for example, were to be grouped: three, two, and one. The more typical arrangement was: seven, five, three. The group therefore consists of an odd number: fifteen. The number of groups is odd: three. And the number of stones within each group is also odd. This technique is called *hacho*, literally, 'to break the harmony.' It in turn created what the gardeners around Kyoto still call *utsuri* (harmonious effect) or *najimi* (familiarity).

The strong religious color of the paradise garden was, of course, lost. This, indeed, would have been what Zen was aiming at. Religion, followers would have said, is larger than its concepts—the truly religious garden would therefore appear areligious to the orthodox eyes of doctrinaire Buddhists. One of the results of this revolutionary religious concept was that the garden, while becoming for the aesthete an object for the most profound contemplation, also became for the first time visible to the common eye. The ordinary man need no longer bother with the involuted symbolism of the mandalistic garden of Estoeric Buddhism. The garden became, in both the highest and lowest sense, in all senses, something to look at.

It is interesting, curious, and worthy of the paradoxes of Zen itself that these gardens, objects of the most profound aesthetic and religious contemplation, should have been often constructed by men who were considered lower than low, the *kawaramono*, or outcasts. These people lived in undesirable places (their name connotes their living along river-banks) and did undesirable work: slaughtering, skinning, well-digging, and so on. Originally, they worked under the *ishitate-so*, or garden-designing priests. In time, however, they themselves became gardeners.

There were at least several reasons that this surprising advance was possible. One was that kawaramono, as the lowest of all classes, had the farthest to rise, and their lot was so unendurable that complacency proved impossible even in so rigid a social order as the Japanese. Another is that they were favored by both the Ashikaga Shoguns and the Zen temples who saw this rise in rank as a way of preventing a real rise in revolt. Another was that Zen, by its nature, both attracted and was attracted to the natural man, the one least hampered by the conventions of a civilized society. The kawaramono might be completely hampered by senseless civilized restrictions but they did not believe in them. They were, essentially and spiritually, free, or ready for freedom.

It was kawaramono who designed one of the gardens at the imperial palace in 1424 and who built the island waterfall in the south garden of Muromachi-dono residence of the Shogun Yoshimitsu (1393–1441) in 1430. They also built the Onryoken garden at Shokokuji in 1439. Two of their number, Hikosaburo and Emon, took part in building a garden at the Madeno-koji residence of the Shogun Yoshimitsu. The famous stone garden at Ryoanji itself may have been designed by outcasts. Undateable—finished sometime between 1499 and 1588—it is ascribed to Soami (d. 1525) and Hosokawa Katsumoto (1430–73), the latter of whom is thought at least to have begun it. At the same time, one of the fifteen stones is signed. There are two names, Kotaro and Seijiro (which may have been pronounced Suejiro or Genjiro), both of which have been identified as those of local gardener-outcasts.

The most famous of the outcasts was Zenami (1389–1482), an adherent of the Jishu sect. To become a priest in this sect was to receive civil rights otherwise withheld from all kawaramono. He stood in high favor both in the sect and in the eyes of the Shogun himself. When he became ill in 1460 it was Yoshimasa who sent him medicine. The connection between the highest man in the land and one of the lowest was that both were aesthetes and that Zenami was also a master gardener.

His main surviving works may be seen at the Onryoken abbot's residence (1458), at the Muromachi Kami Gosho (1476), at the study hall of the imperial palace (1476), and at the Suiin-ken abbot's residence (ca. 1466). In addition, one of his sons, Koshiro, helped rebuild the garden at the Daijo-in abbot's residence in 1498, and Matashiro, Koshiro's son, carried on the line, becoming exceedingly proficient in landscape gardening history, aesthetics, the lore of good and bad luck, and so on.

He and others like him eventually knew more than the Zen priests themselves. As the troubled times continued, it was these former outcasts who carried the honor and the burden of Japan's aesthetic heritage. One Kisen Shusho, living at the Onryoken, seeing this, observed that Zen had fallen upon bad days and that "today's priests know more about slaughter than learning—the pity of it."

In the meantime, during this time of wars and revolts, the contemplative arts continued to prosper. Landscape gardening, having created the stone garden, at the same time was creating a garden even further refined.

Plan of Manshu-in Temple

1 Buddhist hall   5 Island

2 *Shoin*   6 Moss

3 Inner court   7 Stone lantern

4 Dry pond (white sand)   8 Wall

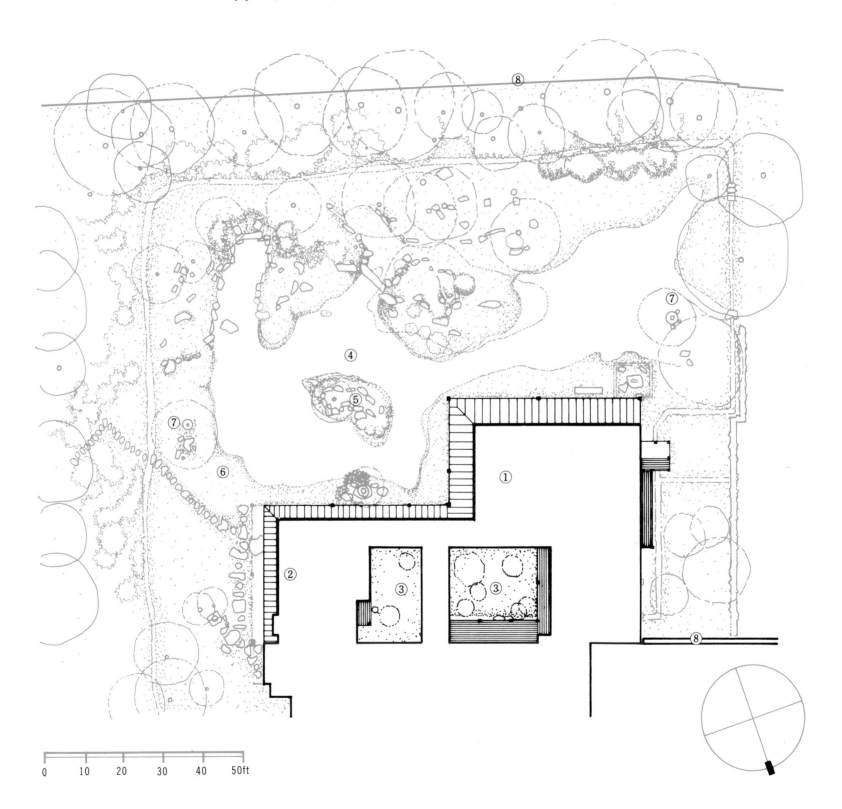

0   10   20   30   40   50ft

The *chaniwa* or tea-garden is a small garden built at the approach to the tea-house or pavilion itself. Such a simple definition, however, affords little conception of the aesthetics, even the philosophy of such a garden.

The tea-ceremony has been compared to the mass in the Catholic liturgy. While such comparison is, admittedly, far-fetched, it does suggest both the purpose and the means of the tea-ceremony. It takes the form of a gathering which is both social and spiritual—a group of people who take tea with a master of the ceremony. It is formal, even solemn. It is a kind of ritual, though it has no designated purpose such as religious rituals have. At the same time, its purpose is clearly spiritual. It is a moment of repose, a time of quiet and selfless aesthetic enjoyment. It is akin to but different from Zen meditation. It resembles it, however, in that the spirit is refreshed, and that the person is that much nearer some perhaps not ultimate, but at any rate further understanding of both himself and his world.

Zen both developed and appropriated the tea-ceremony. One of the higher Zen priests, Ikkyu, went so far as to state that "Buddhism itself is in the tea-ceremony." Just as Zen taught that religion is so omnipresent that a garden, for example, need not concern itself with some pictured mandalistic paradise, so it suggested that the world of the spirit is also omnipresent, and that a moment's quiet contemplation within the pavilion of the tea-master could remind one of this fact.

Besides its spiritual, and hence religious connotations, the tea-ceremony itself was religious. The ceremonies held at the Togu-do in the Higashiyama villa of the Shogun Yoshimasa, did not use the great hall itself. Rather, the ceremony was held in a small room, some six by three feet. This standard-sized room consisting of four and one-half *tatami* mats, that is, six feet three inches by three feet one-half inches, and originally devised by Murata Juko (1423–1502) for the tea-room of his Kyoto retreat, could contain only a few people and was quite independent of any reminder of organized religion.

So was the garden which was attached when the tea-ceremony itself moved from the main buildings. It was small, called *tsubo-no-uchi* (literally 'inside the small garden'), was about ten square yards in size, and was presumed to protect the tea-house, to set it off, and to agree in its studied simplicity with both the house and the ceremony which took place there.

In the early *Yamanoue Soji Ki*, the essays of Yamanoue Soji, the author speaks of a tea-house owned by Takeno Jo (1502–55) to which were attached two tsubo-no-uchi. That in front was three by nine feet; the one on the side was three by twelve feet. The first was designed to be seen from the open windows, an early form of tea-house which did not survive. The second was meant to be walked through on the way to the house itself and may be taken as a prototype of later tea-gardens.

The *Chasho Senrin*, a tea-ceremony manual of the seventeenth century, says that in this garden through which the tea-house is approached "trees should not be planted, nor stones arranged, nor sand scattered, nor gravel designed—for such things distract a person's mind; they confuse and take away the spirituality of the ceremony itself." In Murata's original tea-garden there was but a single willow tree. According to the *Chanoyu Hisho*, another of the early tea-manuals, there was just one maple tree in the garden in front of Matsuya Hisayoshi's tea-pavilion built in 1587. Though shrubs and rocks made an occasional appearance in these early tea-gardens, they sought to follow the saying of an old tea-manual: "A good tea-garden never distracts the heart nor the mind."

Originally, the tea-house had open windows and a veranda, but during the sixteenth century, under the influence of the master aesthete Sen no Rikyu (1522–91), both windows and veranda were eliminated, the result being a small, closed house, creating an environment which fostered the closed and personal atmosphere which so emphasized the spiritual nature of the ceremony. As the house itself became more austere, however, more was allowed into the garden itself. Trees, rocks, shrubs were considered not distracting in their arrangements if the arrangement itself was masterly enough.

This tea-ceremony garden was sometimes called *roji*. This was originally a Buddhist term which connoted 'a spiritual state of perfect selflessness and purity, a state away from the burning mansion of this three-fold world'—the world of desire, the world of form, and the formless world. Such a concept is plainly Buddhist. This world is one of agony— the roji environment was one of bliss, a kind of Buddhist utopia. In this sense the word was first used by Sugiki Fusai (1628–1706) and indicates well the philosophical concept which the garden fulfilled in the Edo period and later.

The word had other connotations, however, both of the major meanings having relevance to the garden itself. It meant 'on the way' or 'while walking.' It also meant 'a narrow alley.' Thus, this usage was equally applicable to those small and narrow gardens, and to the way in which one walked through them in order to reach the place where some ideal or pure state was at least envisioned.

Such a garden was not meant to be simply viewed, as were all of the other gardens we have so far discussed. Indeed, there was no place from which to view it. After Rikyu, and certainly after 1594, the tea-house had only a low and narrow entrance, the *nijiri-guchi*, about two and one-half feet square, and one small window for lighting. The purpose and function of the garden was almost entirely psychological.

It was a space which was attached to the tea-house, spiritually as well as physically. While it might be used for greetings, for such ritual lustrations as washing the hands and rinsing the mouth, its main purpose was to both allow and create that spiritual state which the tea-ceremony itself presumed.

In addition—almost accidentally, it would seem—it was also the first garden to be built sequentially. It was made to walk through, to observe in a certain predetermined order. Historically, one may trace Japanese gardens in general from the paradise garden through the later tour garden, indicating the tea-garden as a necessary middle stage. At the same time, however, it is important in its own right as the first garden to be designed wholly for psychological and aesthetic enjoyment.

Nearly all the makers of these gardens were, as one might expect, also tea-ceremony masters. These men, whether samurai, priests, or tradesmen, shared a series of presumptions about nature and consequently about gardens. The aesthetic is contained in one of the more famous anecdotes about Rikyu. Having once carefully swept his tea-garden and raked all the fallen leaves out of the way, he went to the tree and shook it. Several leaves fell. These he left as they were. It was these leaves which made his garden natural.

One arranged nature but only to an extent, and that extent was gauged by an extremely refined aesthetic sensibility. It was not a question of contrivance; it was a question of control. This control extended in the same direction in which nature itself extended. The desired end was to reduce and hence heighten effect. Flowers were never used in the garden because, since flower arrangements were used within the tea-house itself, blossoms in the garden would detract from the blossoms inside. One makes an effect by reducing; less always means more; a whisper captures attention when a shout cannot. The technique for this was called *sashiai* (literally, 'mutual interference'), and its understanding is central to any comprehension of Japanese aesthetics.

In this regard, one comes upon two words, one of which we met earlier: *sabi* and *wabi*. The former, which was translated as 'patina,' indicates that kind of elegance created by time alone. The elegance of wabi is somewhat different. The wabi quality makes much, indeed, everything, of very little or nothing at all. Its apparent poverty is its salient attribute. Another Rikyu anecdote illustrates the point.

He had a garden in which were growing a large number of marvelous morning-glories. It was arranged that a party come to view them. They arrived early but discovered not one. All had been uprooted and the area was nothing but sand and pebbles. Inside the tea-house, however, arranged in the small alcove, set in a plain holder, was one single, perfect morning-glory. Just as the whole of the garden, the whole nature of all morning-glories everywhere, was contained in that single flower, so, wabi insists, the entire world is found in but one of its varied aspects.

Thus the architecture of the tea-house and the design of the garden itself were purposely rustic, deliberately unostentatious. Man's most 'natural' architecture, that which derived most visibly from nature itself, was considered proper for the house, the environment it sought to create, and the attached garden. Here, beauty was discovered, surprised as it were —a concept called *mitate*, literally, the discovery of a new way of viewing.

To insist upon the perfection of a few fallen leaves, or a single common flower—this led to mitate. Forced to look, led to observe, one suddenly sees, as though with new eyes, a world of beauty in the most ordinary things.

Many qualities went into this—the elegiac feeling of near sorrow, for example, at the realization that this perfection, that leaf, this flower, was already fading, dying; that our world is transient and that evanescence is our lot and our glory. Perhaps such thoughts are also behind the aesthetic canon which held that effects could be made but once.

Basic technique was considered capable of limitless effect, but each effect could be created only once. Imitated beauty was useless beauty. Rikyu, for example, arranged that the trees which he introduced into his tea-garden create an effect of quietude by the taller being near the entrance and the shorter being near the tea-house itself. Furuta Oribe (1543–1615), another tea-master gardener, achieved the same effect by reversing the procedure. As one approached, the trees grew taller, creating a feeling of sheltered peace. The point, however, is that each could be done only once. One approach did not mitigate the other. Both were possible. But they were only possible once. Each master strove to be absolutely different—in the matter of gates, for example: the *saru-do* gate of Rikyu, Oribe's *naka-kuguri* gate, Enshu's *chumon* gate.

Nowadays, of course, tea-gardens are more standardized than not. Just as the original spirit of the tea ceremony itself became attenuated, so both house and garden construction became codified. Today's tea-garden is arranged as follows. It is divided into two portions by a low fence containing a single gate. There is thus an outside roji near the garden gate, an inside roji near the tea-house. In the outer, there is a waiting house, called a *yoritsuki*, where the early guest may wait for those yet to come, and a small toilet called a *setchin*. In the inner there is another rustic shelter where the guests may wait to be summoned. Nearby is a water basin, *tsukubai*, where one washes one's hands, rinses one's mouth. In both sections stone lanterns, *ishi-doro*, are also arranged. There are, in addition, trees—aesthetic concepts having changed to the extent that trees are, far from thought-troubling, considered necessary. Mostly the trees are evergreens, though maple, camellias, and flowering plum are sometimes allowed, as well as, upon occasion, pine, cypress, oak, bamboo, ilex, and various grasses and ferns. The rationale is that there are many ways of preparing both the mind and spirit in producing the feeling that Rikyu once described when he wrote that: "The tea garden is as a passage to a house deep in the mountains. Where there is no path, then the scenery should emerge."

The path is, of course, important. It leads to a state of inner tranquility, and along its length the scenery accommodates and helps create this spiritual serenity. The path itself is made of stepping stones or *tobi-ishi*. Some say that the idea for first using stones came from a fifteenth-century warrior-aesthetician named Ishiguro Dotei, a disciple of Juko, who saw in them merely a way of keeping out of the mud on the way to the tea-house. Another derivation is the story that Rikyu got the idea when he noticed how beautiful the rocks were after a rain.

Together, these anecdotes, found in the *Choando Ki*, or "Essays of Choando" and the *Sawa Shigetsu-shu*, "Essays on the Tea Ceremony," reflect the uses of the stepping stones, which are both practical and aesthetic. They were the two aspects of *watari* (function, literally 'going over') and *kei* (aesthetic appreciation, literally 'scene'). The emphasis put upon one or the other depended entirely upon the man designing the path. Rikyu's design was said to have been about sixty percent watari and forty percent kei, while Oribe's was said to have been the opposite. Thus, properly reasons the early *Roji Kikigaki*, or "Notes on the Roji," Rikyu's way of putting down stepping stones was more functional than Oribe's.

Many varieties of stone may serve as stepping stones. They are chosen for their size, shape, and texture. Most of the stones are natural and uncut, though sometimes especially cut square or round stones are also used.

The usual size is about one and one-half feet in diameter. It is called the *hitotsu-ashi-mono*, or one-step stone. In ordinary gardens, five such stones are to fit into one *ken*, about six and a half feet. The distance between stones is therefore around three inches. This means they are closer together than one can comfortably walk. The result is that the walker moves more slowly and watches where he is going. Since he is thus preoccupied he disregards his surroundings until he arrives at the spot designed for his viewing.

The height of the stone—its *chiri*—again depends upon the designer. Those of Rikyu were two *sun* in height, or about 2.4 inches; those of Kobori Enshu were one *sun*, or 1.2 inches. Usually, the height varied between 1.2 and 3.6 inches, the stone being perhaps wider than that, the height referred to being that distance from the top of the stone to the ground level.

The stones are to be placed in such a way that a freedom of expression is allowed. Precisely, the stones are to express their own nature, and not the gardener's. One such way is the *aiba-no-najimi* in which complimentary stones are arranged side by side, the projecting portion of one stone, for example, facing a hollow section of the next. In order to ensure a proper path, however, Japanese garden designers devised the rule that the path could not be completed until the locality of certain key stones (*yaku-ishi*) was determined. The first stone, the last stone, the *kutsunugi-ishi*, or shoe-removing stone, stones for pausing to view, stones in front of lanterns or water basins—these were all *yaku-ishi*. Once the places for these stones were determined, the other stones were placed in a way which was natural not only to the walker but also to the stones themselves.

In the same way, the other accoutrements—lanterns, basins, trees, shrubs—were so placed that their own nature would be both apparent and expressed and, at the same time, create within the walking viewer that feeling of nature heightened which is the salient quality of the Japanese garden.

The garden as a place of religious meditation became, as we have seen, a place for aesthetic appreciation and, eventually, a place for enjoyment. This last formal phase of the Japanese garden was the *kaiyu-shiki teien*, which might be translated as the 'tour garden,' the garden designed to be walked in. As we have seen, the idea at least partially came from the tea-garden through which the viewer was expected to walk. In the tour garden there was no goal, no tea-house to be reached. Rather, as in many European and American gardens, it was a space of ground designed to be walked about in and the only goal was the pleasure that this afforded. This garden emerged clearly in seventeenth-century Japan during the Edo period (1615–1867), and though composed of various traditional elements it was in itself a new concept.

These tour gardens were very free in both form and pattern. The oldest, the garden of the Katsura Detached Palace, formerly the villa of Prince Hachijo, was described merely as 'a

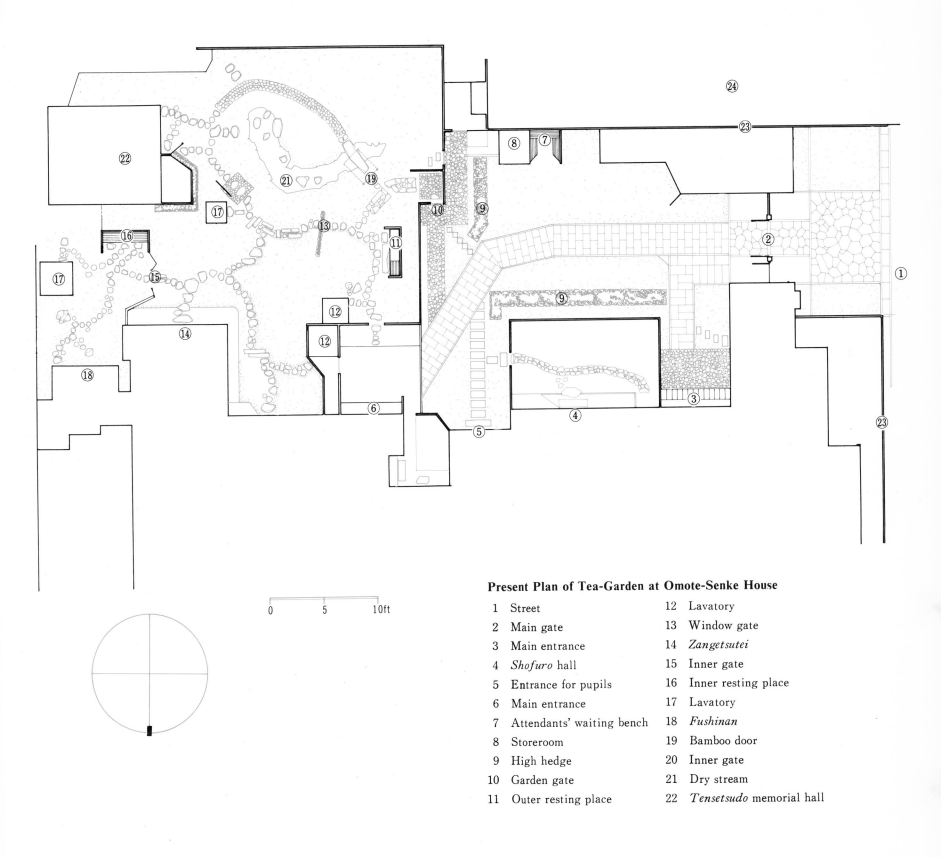

Present Plan of Tea-Garden at Omote-Senke House

1 Street
2 Main gate
3 Main entrance
4 *Shofuro* hall
5 Entrance for pupils
6 Main entrance
7 Attendants' waiting bench
8 Storeroom
9 High hedge
10 Garden gate
11 Outer resting place

12 Lavatory
13 Window gate
14 *Zangetsutei*
15 Inner gate
16 Inner resting place
17 Lavatory
18 *Fushinan*
19 Bamboo door
20 Inner gate
21 Dry stream
22 *Tensetsudo* memorial hall

0   5   10ft

pond surrounded by a footpath,' and is in what we would now call free-form. Equally free are the larger ones—and the tour garden tends by its nature to be quite large—such as that of the Toyamaso villa (ca. 1670) owned by the Tokugawa family of Owari, which extends over an area of three hundred and forty thousand square yards.

To the casual eye such a late tour garden may appear disconcertingly similar to, say, the early paradise gardens at Saihoji or the Golden Pavilion grounds, both of which have lakes and paths as well. The assumptions and implications of these two garden types are, however, quite separate.

In the paradise garden it is not man but Buddha who walks about in this 'paradise' which represents *sanzen-sekai* or 'the whole world.' No matter how a stroller might enjoy this garden, it was not made for his apprehension but for that of the Buddha.

At the same time, the architectural elements of the two gardens are quite different. The tour garden may have shrines or religious halls included—at the Kairaku-en garden of the Toku-gawa family in Mito, for example, there is a small model temple, but it is put there for decoration and not for prayer—but the paradise garden was not nearly so free from the functions of its architectural components. It was built to enhance a temple, just as the tea-garden was built as an adjunct to the tea-house. Absolute gardens, like absolute music, came relatively late in Japan's history.

Too, though the paradise garden had its path and its lake, it had neither philosophy nor rationale regarding the use of the garden. It was the tea-garden which contributed this idea of use and which, in turn, was responsible for the creation of the tour garden. At the same time, too, the gradual secularization of all the arts first allowed and then encouraged an apprehension of nature apart from religious or even aesthetic considerations.

The tour garden, no matter how many buildings it contained, was always arranged around its path, and this path was always arranged around the lake or pond. The direction of the pond was either clockwise, as at the Katsura, or the Koraku-en, or counter-clockwise, as at the Rikugi-en and the Ritsurin-so. Occasionally, in addition, there were branch paths, looping out and returning.

A typical example is the Fukiage garden inside the palace grounds at the site of the old Edo castle in Tokyo, built in 1705 and covering four hundred and fifteen thousand square yards. Along the various paths are, or at one time were: a terrace for viewing Mount Fuji, a man-made hill named Himuro, two shelters, two cottages (one to view the cascades, the other to view the autumn leaves), a rural house, the residence of the Edo village manager, a spring called Fukiage-no-mizu, and so on. All of these were set among paths, groves, thickets, all set about a large pond.

Another example is the Hama Goten (built in 1670 and containing two hundred and eighty-seven thousand square yards) constructed by Tokugawa Tsunashige (1644–78). It contained four man-made hills and four tea-houses. In the Rikugi-en (two hundred thousand square yards in size, built in 1702 by Yanagisawa Yoshiyasu: 1658–1714), all eighty-eight scenic spots mentioned in Japanese classical literature were reproduced.

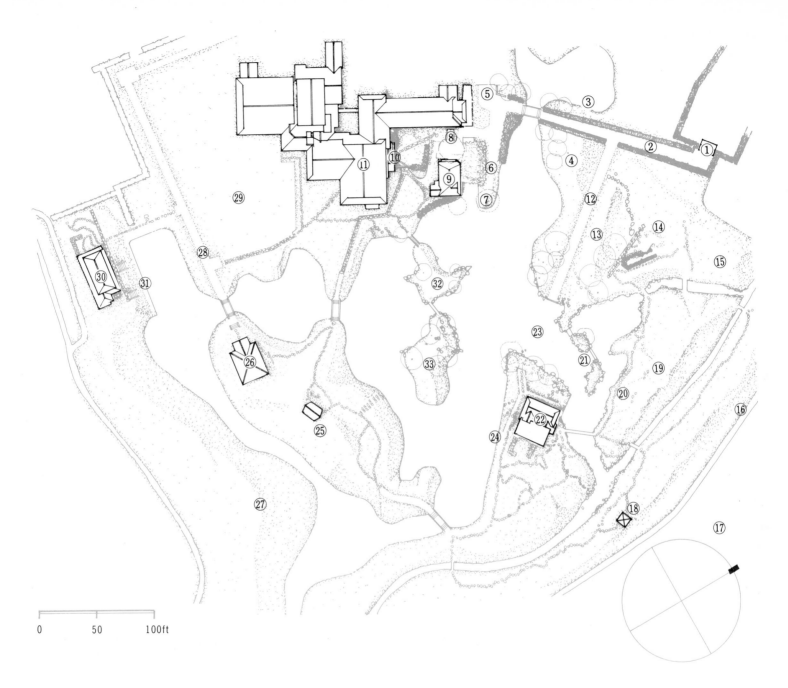

Plan of Garden, Katsura Detached Palace

1 Imperial Gate	10 Entrance	19 Red Pine Hill	28 Riding ground
2 Imperial approach	11 Residence	20 Pondside path	29 Lawn
3 Boat house	12 Riding ground	21 *Amanohashidate*	30 *Shoiken*
4 Maple Mountain	13 *Sotetsuyama* hill	22 *Shokintei*	31 Landing stage
5 Side gate	14 Outer resting place	23 Site of former bridge	32 Island of Immortals
6 Kamenoo Peninsula	15 Flat-topped hill	24 Landing stage	33 *Nakanoshima* island
7 *Sumiyoshinomatsu* pine tree	16 *Ushigase* canal	25 *Shokatei*	
8 Inner gate	17 *Chikurintei* bamboo grove	26 *Onrindo* memorial hall	
9 *Gepparo*	18 *Manjitei*	27 Outer south hill	

The Toyama-so garden was even more elaborate. There were twelve Buddhist halls, eight small temples and shrines, three huts, four roadside tea-stores, four rural houses, four bridges, six gates, four man-made hills, one spring, and one tea-ceremony house—all replicas of those written of in classical literature. In the garden itself there were mountains and a river, on both sides of which were reconstructed the thirty-six buildings of the Odawara post-road station. These included inns, saké and tea-houses, various kinds of stores, a Buddhist hall, an officially appointed inn, and a hall enshrining a master poet named Kakinomoto no Hitomaro.

Such a garden was obviously a world in itself, and illustrates the degree of elaborateness toward which these tour gardens later tended. Perhaps the finest, however, and certainly the most famous, was the first—the garden of the Katsura Detached Palace in Kyoto.

Both garden and villa were completed around 1659 and the work is often accredited to Kobori Enshu, though it was just as probably the work of Hosokawa Yusai, or Prince Toshihito himself, who owned the twenty thousand square foot site.

The placing of the garden and the villa itself is almost theatrically effective. Both buildings and grounds are so rightly placed that wherever you walk, in the rooms, or on the paths, there is a succession of perfect views. Sometimes the garden is oppositely framed by the buildings, sometimes it is the garden which creates a proscenium for a distant wall or roof.

The garden itself is located in front of the three-part main villa. It is filled with ponds, islands, hills, winding paths, rivulets. One may experience it only by walking through it, and proceeding on a course which, roughly circular but with many detours, leads eventually back to the villa. One new view emerges after another. Remembered details of scenes passed merge in unexpected combinations as one pauses and looks back. The other side of the lake, along which one has just come, now seems familiar, yet new, as each turn becomes a revelation, each pause becomes an occasion for new beauty.

Such a continuous landscape garden is then a drama. At Katsura one is spectator at an experience which opens and closes, which speaks and is silent. Or, perhaps, the effect is more like that of music, where surprise can so easily turn into recognition. As in the sonata form there are developments and recapitulations, passages of imitation, and a strong sense of drama. One is carried through this experience as though the course of footpaths had a musical rhythm. From the shadows of the thicket one suddenly emerges upon a spacious view; the sound of rushing waters incites curiosity and imagination; one climbs a slope in the shade and discovers at the crest a sunny panorama which seems vast.

The method of constructing such surprises is called *mie-gakure* (lit. 'seen and hidden'), a gardening technique which deliberately arranges the sights so that they may not be seen in their entirety from any single direction. It is only by moving among them that they may be understood and appreciated. Here unity is found in diversity. In this garden-drama, one becomes the hero oneself because one 'creates' this garden by walking through it. The blueprint is there, and a most cunning one it is, too, but the experience is created by the viewer.

Another technique much used in these later gardens is that of *shakkei* or 'borrowed scenery.' The idea of borrowing a view and incorporating it into a garden was not new. In a sense, it had always existed. A mossy stone brought from deep in the mountains and set up in a town garden brought with it more than itself. It brought the suggestions of the place from whence it had come. An extension of this feeling would suggest the possibility of including the mountains themselves.

Tour gardens, if possible, included at least some of the surrounding scenery. The Edo gardens, for example, incorporated the distant Mount Fuji into the garden composition. Thus, this far-away and soaring peak became a part of the Yokuon-en; of the Sempu-en which belonged to Lord Ishibashi or the Gamo family; of the Toyama-so; of the Naka-yashiki of the Matsudaira family of Aizu; of the Takanawa residence of the Satsuma clan; of the Hama Goten of Tokugawa Tsunashige; and of the Fukiage garden inside the Edo castle.

Another quality of the tour garden, besides its method of construction and its incorporation of distant scenery, was the fact that one's appreciation was considerably enhanced if one had had a good classical education because one was expected to either recognize or provide a suitable literary image. A rewarding walk in the Katsura garden, for example, presumed a thorough knowledge of *The Tale of Genji*, said to have been Prince Toshihito's favorite book and one which had certainly been consulted in determining precisely what was to go into the garden.

In the Koraku-en garden, before its remodeling in 1718, a knowledge of both Japanese classical literature and Chinese Confucian writings was assumed. How else to understand the mixture of elements which resulted in the Bunsho-do hall in which the spirit of the learned Chinese, Bunshosei, was enshrined, the Engetsukyo Bridge, and such Japanese literary allusions as the Togetsu Bridge, and a replica of the bank of the Oi River, all of which contained literary allusions and suggested classical sources?

Both the Rikugi-en and the Ritsurin-so gardens had bridges named Yatsuhashi, after the famous one of classical renown over the Azuma River in the province of Mikawa. Upon crossing the bridge, one stopped to admire the irises planted at its foot. To do so recalled anecdotes concerning Arihara no Narihira, the hero of the *Ise Monogatari*. At the same time one was to remember the bridge-and-iris motif so common to later Japanese decoration. Altogether, the appreciation was to be much deeper than the glancing at bridge and iris would ordinarily afford.

Such pictorial allusion was not, however, completely pedantic. The Yokuon-en villa of 1792 indicated the Matsushima Islands by copying merely two out of existing dozens. When the nine famous pine-viewing scenes were to be brought to mind, none of the nine were actually reconstructed. Instead, a few pines were artfully arranged and these stood for the famous locations with their myriad literary associations. Just as the Japanese have always heightened and refined when copying from nature, so, when copying from art, the merest indication is sufficient.

The tour garden in itself, a combination of art and nature, the last of the great garden styles created or combined by the Japanese, presents, as though in microcosm, the world itself, and in so doing again shows us that particular and peculiar approach to nature which is Japan's own.

From the first gardens to these last gardens, down to the modern gardens of our own age, the Japanese attitude toward nature is revealed as the continuous endeavor to extract the essence of a stone, a tree, a view. In order to do so one recognizes the nature of each, insists upon it, allows this nature to display itself.

The original stone or tree is never natural enough for the Japanese. Rather than working against nature, however, clipping the tree or squaring the stone, the Japanese gardener has from the beginning worked with nature, worked along its grain, as it were. There is pruning and placing but this results in the revealing of a line which nature itself created and then obscured in its own plentitude.

That the Japanese idealize is true enough, but the method of idealization is, as has been indicated, to perceive and then to free that which already exists.

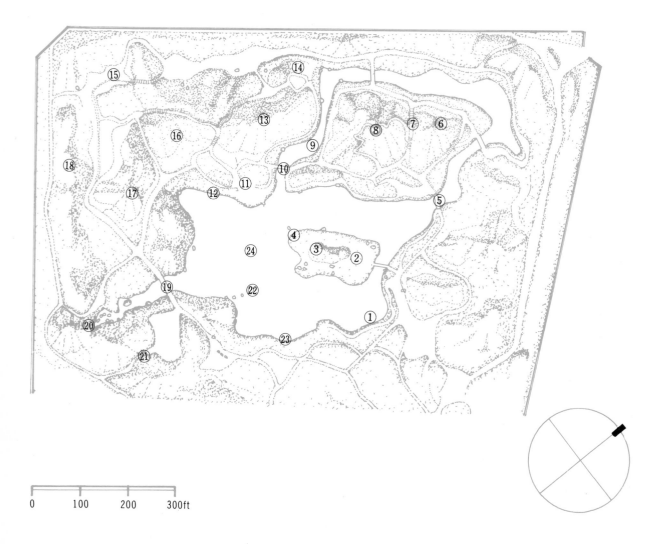

0   100   200   300ft

Plan of Rikugien Garden

1   *Deshiominato* port
2   *Seyama* mountain
3   *Imoyama* mountain
4   *Fukunoume* plum tree
5   *Togetsukyo* bridge
6   *Oinomine* hill
7   *Sennen* slope
8   *Fujishirotoge* pass
9   *Shioji* seaway
10 *Hakuokyo* bridge
11 *Fukiagejaya* tea-house
12 *Fukiagenohama* beach
13 *Fukiagenomine* hill
14 *Tsutsujijaya* tea-house
15 Site of former *Ginkatei*
16 *Minegahana* hill
17 *Koromodegaoka* hill
18 *Shiorigamine* hill
19 *Chidoribashi* bridge
20 *Chinryudo* cave
21 *Shiratorinoseki* barrier
22 *Horaijima* islands
23 *Tamamogaiso* beach
24 Pond

The assumption of this act, as we have seen during the course of this book, is that nature and man are one. By its acceptance of the transitory it emphasizes both the timeless and the instant which is now. By discovering unity in variety, it discovers the forever unique.

In Japan one clearly sees the passing of this philosophy from one generation to another, from one age to the next. It is more than a tradition. It is living thought. And, being alive, it is also variously interpreted.

As the great poet Matsuo Bashō said, centuries ago: one should never imitate that which has been inherited from one's forebears; one should, instead, strive after that for which one's forebears strove.

He was speaking of *haiku*, but he could have been speaking of many things, so common is the attitude expressed. He could have been speaking of gardens, for, no matter the form—paradise garden, tour garden, water garden, sand garden, island garden—behind each is the same attitude toward nature. It is one which remains the same despite its changing forms.

The modern gardener, living in this age of express highways and jet travel, continues to 'strive after that for which one's forebears strove.' It is a belief in the identity of man and nature, one which humbles in its insistence upon the transitory nature of the merely human, but which, at the same time, dignifies by its equal insistence that we are all a part of something larger than ourselves.

2

4

5

11

12

14

21

24

25

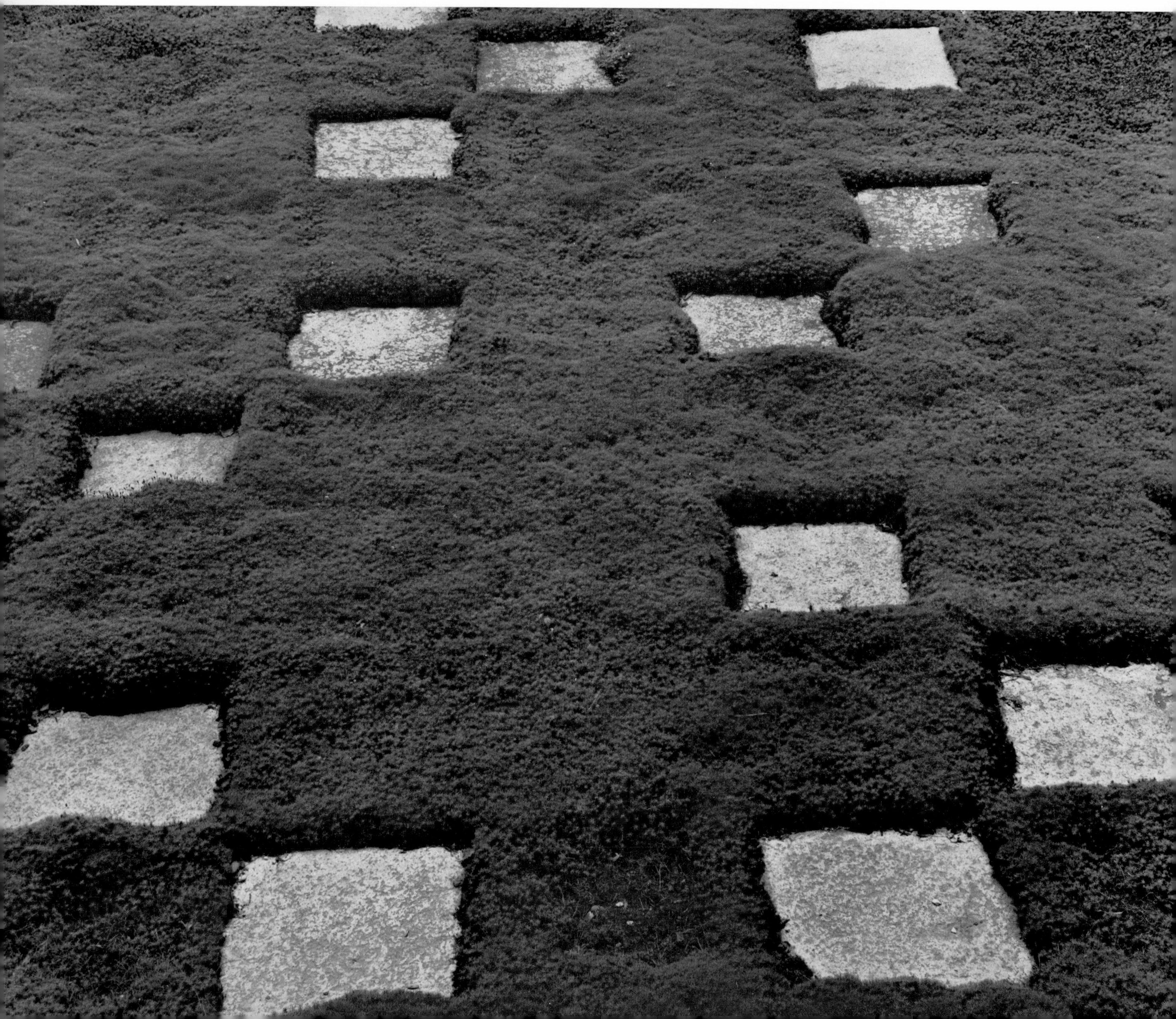

27

31

33

34

37

38

39

42

46

48

55

57

60

127

67

68

69

70

71

72

73

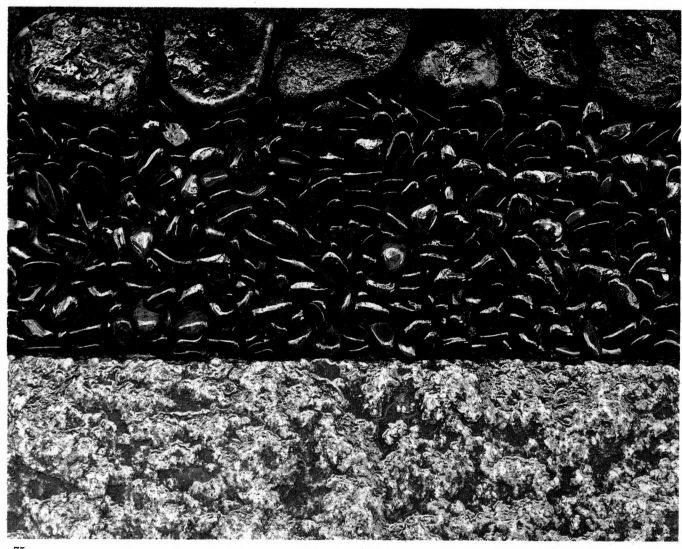

75

76

78

79

83

84

85

149

93

94

95

98

99

100

101

102

103

105

List of Illustrations